Absolute Essentials of Public Relations

Absolute Essentials of Public Relations offers a valuable quick-start introduction to the many facets and forms of public relations theory and practice. It explores contemporary public relations through multiple lenses by focusing on what public relations essentially comprises, how it has come into existence, what contexts public relations works within, what tools and techniques professionals can deploy, and how professionals assess and justify the outcomes of their work.

Divided into two parts – Concepts and Theories, and Applications and Specialisms – the book covers the fundamental theories and concepts and their application in contemporary practice, which together broadly reflect the typical syllabus content for undergraduate, postgraduate, and post-experience introductory courses in public relations. The topics covered in both sections are complemented by mini cases, which showcase academic and professional insights into practice.

Offering a concise and approachable alternative to the mainstream, more heavyweight textbooks available, this book provides a comprehensive introduction to public relations theory and practice.

Danny Moss, PhD, is Emeritus Professor of Corporate & Public Affairs at the University of Chester Business School and Co-Director of the International Centre for Corporate & Public Affairs Research.

Barbara DeSanto, Ed.D, APR, Fellow PRSA, Kansas State University Emeritus Professor, worked in journalism and public relations for 10 years, and spent the next 30 years in the classroom.

Absolute Essentials of Public Relations

Textbooks are an extraordinarily useful tool for students and teachers, as is demonstrated by their continued use in the classroom and online. Successful textbooks run into multiple editions, and in endeavouring to keep up with developments in the field, it can be difficult to avoid increasing length and complexity.

This series of Shortform textbooks offers a range of books which zero-in on the absolute essentials. In focusing on only the core elements of each sub-discipline, the books provide a useful alternative or supplement to traditional textbooks.

Absolute Essentials of Environmental Economics
Barry C. Field

Absolute Essentials of Marketing Research
Bonita M. Kolb

Absolute Essentials of Advertising
Sarah Turnbull

Absolute Essentials of Ethereum
Paul Dylan-Ennis

Absolute Essentials of International Economics
Thomas R. Sadler

Absolute Essentials of Public Relations
Danny Moss and Barbara DeSanto

For more information about this series, please visit: www.routledge.com/Absolute-Essentials-of-Business-and-Economics/book-series/ABSOLUTE

Absolute Essentials of Public Relations

Danny Moss and Barbara DeSanto

LONDON AND NEW YORK

First published 2025
by Routledge
4 Park Square, Milton Park, Abingdon, Oxon OX14 4RN

and by Routledge
605 Third Avenue, New York, NY 10158

Routledge is an imprint of the Taylor & Francis Group, an informa business

British Library Cataloguing-in-Publication Data
A catalogue record for this book is available from the British Library

Library of Congress Cataloging-in-Publication Data
Names: Moss, Danny, 1954– author. | DeSanto, Barbara, 1950– author.
Title: Absolute essentials of public relations / Danny Moss and Barbara DeSanto.
Description: Abingdon, Oxon ; New York, NY : Routledge, 2025. | Series: Absolute essentials of business and economics | Includes bibliographical references and index.
Identifiers: LCCN 2024030603 | ISBN 9780367653392 (hardback) | ISBN 9780367653408 (paperback) | ISBN 9781003129004 (ebook)
Subjects: LCSH: Public relations.
Classification: LCC HD59 .A27 2025 | DDC 659.2—dc23/eng/20240712
LC record available at https://lccn.loc.gov/2024030603

ISBN: 978-0-367-65339-2 (hbk)
ISBN: 978-0-367-65340-8 (pbk)
ISBN: 978-1-003-12900-4 (ebk)

DOI: 10.4324/9781003129004

Typeset in Times New Roman
by Apex CoVantage, LLC

Contents

List of figures vii
List of tables viii
List of boxes ix
About the authors xi
List of contributors xii

Introduction 1
BARBARA DESANTO AND DANNY MOSS

PART 1
Concepts and theories: what is public relations: definitions and disciplinary boundaries? 3

1 **Defining public relations** 5
BARBARA DESANTO

2 **Models, role and scope of public relations** 18
DANNY MOSS

3 **Public relations practitioner roles** 26
DANNY MOSS

4 **Public relations and communications strategy** 37
DANNY MOSS

5 **Public relations ethics and professional standards** 50
MELANIE POWELL

PART 2

PR applications and specialisms 61

6 **Corporate communication** 63
DANNY MOSS

7 **Public relations and marketing** 76
DANNY MOSS

8 **Internal/employee communication** 88
CARL HOLLOWAY

9 **Crisis management** 99
BARBARA DESANTO

10 **Public relations and public affairs** 112
PETER OSBORNE

11 **International public relations** 123
BARBARA DESANTO

12 **Public relations and social media** 132
REBECCA DICKENSON AND NATALIE ELVIN

Index *147*

Figures

2.1a Four Models of Public Relations 19
2.1b The Four Models of Public Relations Positioned on Professional and Craft PR Practice Continua 21
2.2 The Potential Operating Environments and Forces Shaping the Role of PR 24
3.1 Composite View of the PR Practitioner's Manager-Technician Roles 28
3.2 A Day in the Life of a PR 'Technician' 33
3.3 A Day in the Life of a Senior PR Manager 34
4.1 RACE Model 43
4.2 Grunig and Repper's Seven-Stage Strategic Planning Model 45
4.3 CMACIE Model for the Strategic Management of Public Relations 47
9.1 Stages in Crisis Management 103
10.1 The Nexus of Business, Government Interests and the Mediating Role of Public Affairs /Communication 114

Tables

3.1	Defining Practitioner Skills, Knowledge, Personal Attributes, and Competencies	30
3.2	Inventory of Practitioner Skills, Knowledge, and Personal Attributes	31
4.1	Mintzberg's 5Ps of Strategy	39
4.2	Summary of Key Concepts, Frameworks, Schools of Thought about Management Strategy	40
4.3	Strengths and Weaknesses of RACE Model	44
5.1	Overview of Ethical Perspectives (6Ps)	52
5.2	Ethics and Key Steps in the PR Planning Process	57
5.3	Ethical Decision-making	58
6.1	Example of a Typical Issues–Stakeholder Matrix	67
6.2	Corporate PR/Corporate Communication Activities/Tools	73
7.1	Comparison of Marketing and PR: Key Distinguishing Characteristics	80
8.1	Breakdown of Workforce Statistics for NHS in the UK 2023	91
9.1	Newsom Crisis Typology	102
11.1	Hofstede's Cultural Dimensions	126
11.2	Selected International Public Relations Frameworks	127

Boxes

1.1 Essentials summary 5
1.2 Examples of academic and industry body definitions of public relations 7
1.3 Examples of practitioner definitions of public relations 8
2.1 Essentials summary 18
2.2 Buffering and bridging in action: the Volkswagon emissions case 23
3.1 Essentials summary 26
4.1 Essentials summary 37
4.2 Definitions of strategy 38
5.1 Essentials summary 50
6.1 Essentials summary 63
6.2 Definitions of CC that focus on the idea of CC as a strategic management function 64
6.3 Corporate reputation 70
7.1 Essentials summary 76
7.2 Definition of marketing 78
7.3 Iceland's palm oil initiative 81
7.4 Dove # The Selfie Talk campaign 85
8.1 Essentials summary 88
8.2 Our definition of internal communication 89
8.3 Herzberg's motivation and hygiene factor theory 92
8.4 Organisational culture 94
8.5 Examples of issues/problem scenarios typically handled by IC communicator 95
8.6 Communication audits 97
9.1 Essentials summary 99
9.2 Oklahoma City Bombing 1995 100
9.3 Coombs' crisis communication channel preparation best practices 107
9.4 Where the crisis happens 108
9.5 Coombs' initial crisis response practice points 109

9.6 Coombs' post-crisis-phase best practices 110
10.1 Essentials summary 112
10.2 Lobbying 113
10.3 A public affairs strategy in practice – how a UK private water company's public affairs function harnessed issues management to stem deep reputational damage 120
11.1 Essentials summary 123
11.2 International stakeholder analysis for targeting in India 125
11.3 Two American soft drinks make hard landings 128
11.4 BMW sings the blues 129
12.1 Essentials summary 132
12.2 Trends in social media usage 134
12.3 Thought leadership 135
12.4 Using AI 136
12.5 Influencer types 139
12.6 Aldi's #FreeCuthbert campaign 141
12.7 Social media evaluation metrics 143

About the authors

Danny Moss, PhD, is Emeritus Professor of Corporate & Public Affairs at the University of Chester Business School and Co-Director of the International Centre for Corporate & Public Affairs Research. He has played a leading role in establishing master's level education in public relations in the UK at the University of Stirling and then at Manchester Metropolitan University and the University of Chester. He was one of the co-founders of the Bled PR Research Symposium and co-founder and co-editor of the Journal of Public Affairs and has authored and edited many books, journal articles, and conference papers.

Barbara DeSanto, Ed.D., APR, Fellow PRSA, Kansas State University Emeritus Professor, worked in journalism and public relations for 10 years, and spent the next 30 years in the classroom. She has authored journal articles exploring the nature of public relations work in different environments and has collaborated with Dr. Danny Moss, University of Chester, on several books about public relations management and international public relations cases.

Contributors

Natalie Elvin is a freelance marketing strategist and copywriter. Before launching her business in 2020, Natalie worked for the University of Leeds in events, comms, and digital education roles. She works on campaigns for her direct clients as well as collaborating with other consultants and white labelling for digital agencies.

Rebecca Dickenson has a master's degree in Journalism and has spent the past 15 years working in journalism and communications. She has worked in both in-house and agency public relations roles, delivering traditional and digital campaigns for B2B and consumer clients across a wide range of sectors. She now runs her own comms consultancy, delivering PR, social media, digital and influencer campaigns.

Carl Holloway is a director of communications with experience across education, health, local authority, and social housing. He holds master's degrees in Strategic Communication and Management Practice as well as the AMEC Certificate in PR Measurement and Evaluation. He has a passion for raising the profile of Public Relations as a strategic management function.

Peter Osborne, a former journalist, has more than 30 years of communications experience in highly demanding and sensitive PR environments including nuclear, water, electricity, environment, and health and social care – across the private, public, and third sectors.

Peter has managed all aspects of public relations including media relations, public affairs, international relations, and internal communications for organisations including BNFL, United Utilities, Keep Britain Tidy, Interserve, and the largest provider of health and social care services based in the north-west of England, Alternative Futures Group.

Peter holds a master's degree (MA) in Public Relations and a first degree in Economics and Economic and Social History (BA 2:1).

Melanie Powell, MPhil, FCIPR, is an experienced Public Relations educator, now teaching CIPR professional qualifications online since retiring from Manchester Metropolitan University in 2023. Previously, she was a senior lecturer in Public Relations at MMU and Leeds Beckett University. Before becoming an academic, she worked as a practitioner in local authority public relations and arts marketing.

Introduction

Barbara DeSanto and Danny Moss

Public relations (PR) has and is still often misunderstood, misrepresented, and even demonised as the tool of 'Machiavellian manipulation', associated with political spin doctoring or corporate cover-up. Even where when not viewed in such negative terms, its potential to contribute significantly to an organisation's strategic success is all too often overlooked and in many cases, it is treated as a troubleshooting resource of last resort, a sort of communication orphan stashed in a glass case on the hallway wall with a banner reading 'In case of emergency, break glass'.

Paradoxically, if quizzed about whether they have heard of public relations, most might reply in the affirmative, but if pressed further to define what it is, they might struggle to come up with an answer. Indeed, even professionals and academics working in PR have yet to agree on a consensus definition. Yet despite such definitional problems, organisations of all shapes and sizes are continually engaged in a wide array of activities that shape perceptions of that organisation, which impact the organisation's reputation. Even if not recognised as such, all this outward- and inward-facing activity is, in essence, a form of public relations. Here, the question is, does the organisation want to try to manage this PR-related activity or not?

The *Absolute Essentials of Public Relations* offers an overarching introduction to the many facets and forms of public relations practice, including corporate communication, marketing and PR, employee communication, and public affairs and related specialised areas of crisis communication and media relations. Each chapter explores a specific area of public relations practice through a broadly similar four-part framework: first, considering how the specific location of public relations is defined/its distinctive characteristics; then examining the relevant stakeholders that will typically be the main focus for that area of practice; prior to exploring the range of issues/challenges that are usually encountered; and finally, examining the type of communication/PR tools or activities that tend to be deployed to address those issues.

We intend that this introduction to public relations will encourage you to explore more deeply the critical role that public relations as an ethical, well-managed form of two-way communication can – and should – play in an organisation, no longer an orphan discipline but a full-fledged sibling.

DOI: 10.4324/9781003129004-1

Part 1

Concepts and theories

What is public relations: definitions and disciplinary boundaries?

1 Defining public relations

Barbara DeSanto

Box 1.1 Essentials summary

The search for a single universally agreed definition of public relations (PR) has proved elusive with some studies identifying nearly 500 different definitions of public relations. Hence, rather than looking for one definition, it is much more useful to try to distinguish the recurring themes found within definitions. Here, more of a consensus emerges with P being recognised as focused on the task of 'communication management', using 'two-way communication' programmes as the basis for 'managing relationships' with relevant stakeholder groups often termed 'publics'. A key challenge for public relations scholars and practitioners has been to combat the negative connotations that often surround PR, notably in terms of its association with propaganda and manipulation of opinion, which can be traced to the early ideas advanced by Edward Bernays in terms of his notion of 'engineering of consent'. How PR is understood will depend not only on whose perspective we are considering and what preconceptions and prejudices they may hold about it but also on the environment/context in which PR is viewed. Here, perceptions of PR may vary with the type of organisation, its history and traditions, the industry sector, and even the type of functional department where public relations is located. Understanding of public relations may also differ across geographic boundaries with differences in the socio-economic, political, and media landscape shaping the way PR is understood and practised. Clearly arriving at a definition and understanding of what we mean by the term public relations is a fundamental starting point in exploring wider questions about what role the function can play in an organisational and societal context.

DOI: 10.4324/9781003129004-3

Defining public relations

This book explores and explains public relations (PR) as a professional practice and field of academic study. The book's various chapters will examine public relations' role in contemporary society and business, what it comprises as a practice, and how it fits into the broader organisational, business, political, and social context. This is a challenging task as there are numerous ways and contexts in which public relations can manifest itself and interact with different stakeholders. Furthermore, explaining PR requires addressing and overcoming the various stereotypes and prejudices often surrounding it, perhaps most notably the widespread presumption that public relations is almost synonymous with the notion of propaganda. Indeed, the classical description of public relations advanced by one of the earliest PR protagonists, Sigmund Freud's nephew Edward Bernays (1947), is that professional PR is concerned essentially with the 'engineering of consent'. This term has been twisted and misinterpreted to associate PR with a form of nefarious manipulative activity. In contrast, Bernay explained that 'professional public relations activities are planned and executed by trained practitioners by scientific principles, based on the findings of social scientists'. He likened this approach to that of professional engineers who draw on the physical sciences.

However, perceptions of PR as a manipulative activity having negative connotations with wartime propaganda have continued to plague perceptions of PR not just in Western developed economies and countries where arguably PR has become firmly established, but evidence of these negative associations can be found in countries around the world not only amongst the general public but also within business and political circles.

Even offering a clear and widely accepted definition of public relations is more complex than one might expect. Indeed, over the years, many attempts have been made to identify a universal definition of public relations that would locate it within a relevant social and business context. Many of these definitions have been criticised as amounting to little more than rather bland 'slogans'. A plethora of scholarly articles have addressed this problem; a short reading list is included at the end of this chapter. Here, for example, Rex Harlow, albeit working in the late 1970s, found some 472 'definitions' from which he sought to distil public relations into one all-encompassing statement, which in essence defined public relations as *a distinctive management function which helps establish and maintain mutual lines of communication, understanding, acceptance and cooperation between an organisation and its publics*.

Similarly, several professional associations in public relations, like the US-based Public Relations Society of America (PRSA) and the UK-based Public Relations and Communications Association (PRCA), advanced similar but different definitions. Attempting to pull all of the concepts, different types of practice contexts, and nuances into one all-encompassing definition of public relations is a nearly impossible task. Arguably, what is a more achievable goal is to distil some of the core ideas that tend to recur across the range of definitions/descriptions of public relations. Here, notions such as 'managed communication', 'relationship-building', 'two-way communication', 'image and reputation building', and 'stakeholder communication' feature in many definitions, but it is the notion of public relations being about the 'management of communication' between an organisation and relevant stakeholders that is perhaps the most powerful recurring theme. Thus, for example, in their seminal textbook, Grunig and Hunt (1984) define public relations concisely as the function responsible for the *management of communication between an organisation and its publics*. Of course, while perhaps simply stated, this definition raises questions about what *managing communication* involves? What sort of *communication* are we referring to, and who are the *publics*? The lack of a simple answer to these questions is why defining public relations can be problematic.

Some typical examples of how public relations has been defined by academics as well as by professionals working in the industry are summarised in Boxes 1.2 and 1.3.

Box 1.2 Examples of academic and industry body definitions of public relations

Grunig and Hunt (1984)

'Public relations is the management of communication between an organisation and its publics.' *Managing Public Relations*. Holt, Rinehart, and Winston: New York, NY.

Cutlip, Center, and Broom (2009)

> *A management function that establishes and maintains mutually beneficial relationships between an organization and the publics on whom its success or failure depends.*

The public relations society of America (PRSA)

> *Public relations is a strategic communication process that builds mutually beneficial relationships between organisations and their publics.*

Https://prsa.org/learnaboutpublicrelations.
Retrieved 20 September 2023

The chartered institute of public relations

> *Public relations is about reputation – the result of what you do, what you say and what others say about you. Public relations is the discipline which looks after reputation, with the aim of understanding and support and influencing opinion and behaviour.*
>
> https://www.cipr.co.uk. Retrieved 20 September 2023

Here, it might be interesting to compare these more academic and industry body definitions with some examples of the more thoughtful practitioner definitions, which interestingly contain many of the same arguments and principles found in the academically framed definitions.

Box 1.3 Examples of practitioner definitions of public relations

> *Public Relations is a strategic communications process that sets out to build and maintain mutually beneficial relationships between two or more parties.*
>
> (Matias Rodsevich, CEO, PR Lab, www.prlab.co.uk)

Public relations is communicating your organisation's messages at the right time and in the right place to the right audience. With the proliferation of tools and technologies, we can measure the value of those efforts and how they align with a business's overall mission. (Marla Aaron – MRM Worldwide, www.mrm-mccann.co.uk)

> *Public relations is the practice of understanding the purpose of an organisation and its relationships within society. It is the planned and sustained activity of engagement between these two parties to influence behaviour change, and build mutual understanding and **trust.** Engagement between an organisation and its publics is the core of public relations practice. It is a two-way process by which an organisation communicates with its publics and vice versa.*
>
> (Stephen Waddington, Chief Engagement Officer at Ketchum 2021, www.Ketchum.com)

Public relations is the art of creating lasting relationships, based on respect and truth, between interdependent entities existing in the public domain. *PR has nothing to do with manipulation, twisting the reality, smearing competitors or political opponents, or praising made up qualities of products, services, parties, or public figures. PR teaches you the principles of correct exchange of information between individuals and companies* (Grzegorz Szczepański, CEO at Hill+Knowlton Strategies Poland, http://hkstrategies.pl/pl/H-K-Strategies/).

Source: Cohen, H. (2011). '31 Public Relations Definitions'. <heidicohen.com/public-relations-definitions/> Accessed 17 February 2024

Deconstructing the definitions

As was suggested earlier, a number of recurring themes can be discerned from a synthesis of the many definitions of public relations, notably around such notions as 'managed communication', publics, and 'relationship-building/management', and of course, 'communication' – terms that arguably require some further explanation.

Managed communication embraces the idea of deliberate and planned communication programmes in which those initiating the communication have a clear appreciation of who they are targeting, what are the desired outcomes with respect to each target, and hence what needs to be communicated to those targets. Of course, managing communication programmes is not always as straightforward as it might appear in terms of the classic management processes of planning, organising, directing, and controlling communication activities. In reality, management of any function can be a relatively complex, nuanced, and sometimes extremely problematic activity as it attempts to direct, organise, and control the work and behaviour of individuals or groups of workers who may not always act as intended. However, it is also essential to recognise that managed communication also embraces the need for systematic 'listening' to all relevant stakeholders to understand and respond to any legitimate issues they might have. In other words, managed communication involves a two-way process; the penultimate element of which involves the design of appropriate messages and the selection of the most effective channels of communication through which to deliver these messages. Finally, as with any programme of action, it is essential to monitor and evaluate the outcome and whether the intended goals have been achieved. A further examination of public relations planning and management can be found in Chapter 4.

Publics is the term generally used in public relations to refer to those individuals, groups, or organisations that form the key targets for any public relations engagement/activity. 'Publics' may consist of those who hold significant power or influence vis-à-vis an organisation, whose support is needed or whose opposition needs to be combatted. Equally, in a commercial context, the publics might comprise people whose support or custom is sought through a programme of persuasive communication. The term publics is often confused with that of 'stakeholders' or simply 'target audiences'. The latter is the term more commonly used in marketing and advertising rather than public relations because it implies a 'passive' target group whose purchasing behaviour, marketing, or advertising activity is intended to influence in favour of the communicating organisation. The terms 'stakeholders' and publics are often used almost synonymously, and although closely aligned, they do differ particularly from a PR planning perspective. In short, stakeholders refer to those individuals or groups who have a direct or indirect 'stake' in an organisation, and the actions of either stakeholders or the organisation can have consequences for each other. Publics are that subset of stakeholders directly engaged with the specific issues or challenges the organisation is addressing, and who are likely to be directly affected by the organisation's policies/actions, or whose own actions threaten to frustrate or completely derail the organisation's intended goals and actions. As a consequence, it is the publics who are normally the primary targets for any PR programme of action. The concept of stakeholders and publics is central to all aspects of PR theory and practice and thus recurs throughout this book.

Relationship-building/management is a term that has become increasingly popular in a wide array of functional and social contexts ranging from marketing HRM and communication to the sciences and from politics to healthcare. Everyone seems to recognise the importance of building and maintaining 'relationships' between relevant groups, institutions, or even nations. Indeed, the term 'Relationship Management' emerged in the latter quarter of the 20th century and was hailed as some 'new science' of doing things. Here, for example, 'relationship marketing' emerged in the early 1990s (e.g. Christopher et al. 1991). The relationship management perspective of public relations emerged in the early 2000s (Leadingham & Bruning 2000), focusing on exploring those relationship dimensions upon which good organisation–public relationships are initiated, developed, and maintained. Here, it might be argued that this 'relationship perspective' is nothing new from that which has always been at the heart of public relations, namely understanding who it is [the publics] that is most important to the successful achievement of the organisation's goals and ensuring that organisations engage effectively with them to maintain and enhance their support/custom/loyalty, or minimise of assuage their opposition. The relationship perspective focuses on analysis of the relationship-building and maintenance *process*, emphasising the need to identify and understand those variables that have the most significant influence on the quality of each relationship. Moreover, critical to the success of any relationship is the development and maintenance of effective communication between the parties involved, hence the importance of the public relations role in this context.

Communication is often viewed as essentially what lies at the heart of public relations; it is the voice and actions of an organisation, including symbols, words, and activities that individually and collectively represent a picture of that organisation to different groups that matter to it.

Thus, 'communication' can take a wide array of different forms in terms of both messages and channels. Messages can be visual, oral, and written, or a combination of these. Messages can be delivered through an increasingly diverse range of media channels extending well beyond the traditional print, broadcast, or visual display channels to embrace contemporary Internet and social media channels that have become the dominant media through which the younger generations, particularly, communicate. When examining public relations communication, one important distinction is between one-way and two-way communication which is often referred to in academic debate as 'asymmetrical' and 'symmetrical' communication. One long-standing controversy surrounds arguments about the effectiveness of one-way and two-way communication. Here, perhaps the most well-known advocate of the efficacy of symmetrical communication is James Grunig (Grunig & Hunt 1984; Grunig & Grunig 1992), who argued that symmetrical communication in the form of open dialogue between the parties involved directed towards genuine problem-solving based on a willingness to listen to the other party's arguments and work towards a mutually agreed outcome is a core characteristic of 'excellently' managed communication and excellently managed organisations. Here, Grunig (1992) argued that terms such as trust, credibility, employee-centred communication, relationships, reciprocity, tolerance for disagreement, and negotiation pervade the literature. However, this symmetrical model of organisational communication has come under considerable criticism as representing a far too idealised view of how the majority of organisations behaved with respect to communicating with their stakeholders in real-world scenarios. In a subsequent reflective and essentially conciliatory article, Grunig (2006) acknowledged that examples of pure symmetrical communication might rarely be found, particularly in an often highly competitive business world. He suggested a more appropriate if still somewhat aspirational notion of 'cultivating' or 'bridging strategies' might better explain the behaviour of organisational management teams in today's often challenging domestic and international business world. Grunig suggests that these terms better capture how organisations often seek to adapt to and build relationships with relevant stakeholder groups through two-way communication that essentially seeks to balance stakeholder and/or organisational interests.

Of course, perceptions and understanding of public relations will invariably depend on who is being asked to define it. As was suggested earlier, public relations is often referred to in a quite negative, pejorative manner, especially within media circles. Here, White and Park (2010) reported on the consistent negative stereotypical themes found in the way public relations has been and continues to be portrayed within the media. They pointed to a range of studies that found public relations described in terms of such themes as 'damage control', 'publicity', 'an attempt to hide or disguise the truth', and 'attempts to advance a company's agenda at others' expense' (White & Park 2010).

One definition

So, having acknowledged the multiplicity of definitions of public relations that exist, do we need to settle on a single definition, or is it sufficient to acknowledge the key themes that recur within many of the definitions? While no one definition will necessarily satisfy all commentators, academics, or professionals, it is probably not unreasonable to suggest that a broad consensus might be found around the key themes of 'communication management', 'relationship-building', 'the central importance of stakeholders/publics', and the 'development and maintenance of effective two-way communication'.

Of course, having a definition of any concept serves a number of valuable purposes, not the least clarifying the meaning of what we are discussing and allowing a better understanding of the concept. As highlighted earlier, public relations has a long track record of being misunderstood and confused with other communication-related concepts, such as marketing communication and publicity, or more notoriously, propaganda.

Thus, before exploring other important aspects of public relations work and its role in business and society, we have constructed a working definition of public relations, synthesised from the many different definitions we have unearthed.

Our working definition of public relations

> *Public relations is the ethical management of organisational communication to engage, build and sustain mutually beneficial relationships with strategically important stakeholders.*

Having explored the complex 'minefield' of definitions of public relations, drawing out the most prominent and significant themes that explain public relations as a distinctive organisational function, it remains for us to explore some of the most common scenarios and contexts in which organisations may turn to the public relations function for assistance and support.

Scenarios in which organisations often turn to public relations

While arguably public relations should have a constant presence, proactively scanning the organisation's environment for any potential threats or opportunities that might impact the organisation's direction and ability to achieve its goals, in reality, public relations appears to be called upon in some scenarios more so than others. These scenarios seem to include typically:

- When an organisation has come under intense media scrutiny and attracted potentially damaging media coverage
- When an organisation is experiencing a crisis of some form or another

- When an organisation needs to raise its profile and improve its external image
- When an organisation is going through a significant restructuring or re-branding exercise and needs to strengthen internal bonds and a sense of identity among employees
- Perhaps most commonly, when public relations is called on to support marketing and sales operations to create a more receptive environment for the more explicit sales and marketing messaging.

Of course, these are not the only scenarios in which public relations is called into action, but what they do reflect is perhaps an overemphasis on the reactive use of public relations to firefight a problem or redress a situation that has developed unexpectedly rather than the use of a more proactive approach in which public relations plays what is sometimes termed a '*boundary spanning*' role, continually scanning the organisation horizon to pick up on and anticipate any issues that might otherwise blow the organisation off course as well as anticipating valuable opportunities to help position the organisation to take advantage of emerging trends. This boundary scanning responsibility is arguably one of the most important ways in which public relations can contribute to the organisation's longer-term strategic development and how, if allowed to do so, it earns its place at the senior management table. We return to this argument in Chapter 5 when examining the strategic role of public relations.

Context and environment

As suggested earlier, people's perceptions of public relations can and do vary considerably often depending on their own experiences of public relations, either directly at work or as a result of what they have read or heard about PR – its image and reputation. And, of course, images and longer-term reputations are created and shaped not only by direct experience but are often the product of an array of different stimuli and influences, many of which may come from second-hand sources, often most significantly nowadays what is being said on social media. Thus, in many cases, perceptions of public relations will have been framed and shaped by often quite negative and even hostile media coverage. As most PR professionals acknowledge, public relations and journalism are, at best, uncomfortable 'bed-fellows', and their relationship is often characterised as an uneasy symbiotic one.

In many organisations, the senior executives may have had limited direct exposure to PR, and many will almost certainly have had little, if any, experience of specific PR training. In such cases, the PR professional may face an uphill battle to convince the senior management in their organisation of the potential value of PR. Thus, when organisations encounter challenging 'scenarios', PR may have a chance to 'shine' and establish its credibility and value to the organisation in question.

Industry sector and organisational influences

Examining other context-related influences on how PR is understood, there seems to be plenty of anecdotal evidence to suggest that both the type of organisation and industry/sector in which it is based can exert a strong influence on how the PR function is positioned, resourced, and what power/influence it can exercise. Thus, in highly competitive, marketing-orientated FMCG industries and companies, where marketing and advertising often lead the way in decision-making circles, PR might be relegated to playing a largely secondary publicity role. In contrast, in highly regulated industry sectors such as oil, energy, water, and transport, where companies may have to compete for licences to operate and are often under considerable regulatory and public scrutiny, maintaining positive relationships with the industry regulatory body and with the customer base and its representatives may be critical to the longer-term retention of operating licenses and hence the financial success of the company. In this context, PR and its associated sub-function of public affairs may play a vital role in ensuring the company's overall mission and strategies are understood and any opposition from political and pressure group sources is as far as possible neutralised.

Similarly, in some industries/organisations, there may be strong values and prejudices about which functions are critical to the organisation's success and thus deserve a 'seat at the top table'. Here, PR might well be seen as of lesser importance and, even worse, a 'necessary evil' in terms of the resources devoted to it. This type of situation and associated prejudices are perhaps more commonly found in older traditional industries such as engineering, industrial manufacturing, and banking, where PR may have rarely, if ever, had a seat at the top table. However, even in such traditional industry settings, the 'tide has been turning' as such industries are opened up to greater scrutiny and are pressured to become more transparent in their actions and policies. Also, with increasing globalisation, the need for improved communication with what might be a very diverse and geographically dispersed internal and external stakeholder audience has placed ever more emphasis on the need for an effective PR/communication function.

In recent years, cost-cutting pressures and the digital transformation of many areas of work have seen the severe downsizing or even closure of many specialists in house PR departments, and only the very largest corporation/organisation tend to have specialist public affairs or employee communication teams where their cost might then be justified. Increasingly, the trend seems to be for organisations to have a relatively small in-house team of PR/communication people, who are expected to fulfil a range of different roles, perhaps supported by freelancers or external agencies when particular circumstance dictates that the in-house team requires additional support.

The declining number and/or size of in-house PR/communication departments has not helped in understanding the nature and role of public relations in today's fast-changing business, media, and social world. Moreover, the inconsistency in how these departments are titled arguably only adds to the confusion that may already exist. Indeed, it is increasingly difficult to come across many in-house PR/communication departments that are still called 'Public Relations'. This is almost certainly down to the negative connotations that have been associated with the term 'public relations', and so terms such as 'Corporate Communication', 'Public Affairs', or 'Strategic Communication Management' have become increasingly commonplace to describe in-house departments and even more so with the senior executives who are in charge of these departments with few if any having the term 'public relations' in their official title. Ironically, when questioned about what they and their departments do, the response will often include recognition that they manage the organisation's public relations strategies and activities.

International influences

The increasing internationalisation of many industries and opening up of many markets and trading blocks to international competition have also increased emphasis on how all the 'players' involved communicate and respond to the changing demands of what is for many industries these days an international/global audience. Indeed, it is perhaps a bit of a cliché, but it is true that the world of business and communication is global, and what happens in the West may be very quickly replicated elsewhere. Here, the Internet has been a huge factor shaping the nature of domestic and international trading and competition for many sectors on an unprecedented scale. Consequently, many organisations have recognised the need and challenge of managing communication across potentially diverse stakeholder and customer audiences. Here, the need to build a profile, and to understand cultural, language media, and potentially regulatory differences is a challenge that PR/communication professionals in their 'boundary spanning' role are arguably well placed to address. Of course, the additional challenge in this international setting is that the background training and expertise required to perform the often sensitive communication role are not always readily available. Indeed, in some regions, PR is still little understood or even recognised as such, and hence, organisations seeking to operate in such regions and extend their PR/communication strategies have to either bring expertise in from elsewhere or train up local staff, or in some cases, hire international communication agencies with a local presence to adapt and deliver their strategies on the ground. Understanding what is possible and acceptable in terms of communication strategies in different national and regional markets is critically important to developing an effective public relations/communication strategy for each area. This fascinating and challenging topic of international public relations is one that we explore further in Chapter 11.

Concluding comments

As we have sought to demonstrate in this chapter, there is no one universal definition or understanding of public relations. Rather there are numerous definitions which contain a number of recurring and central themes that help us make sense of what public relations is and what role it might play within and on behalf of organisations as well as in society. The notions of a function concerned with managing communication, using two-way communication to build and sustain relationships with relevant stakeholders/publics continue to recur in attempts to define and explain public relations. However, as we have acknowledged, one of the chief obstacles to achieving any universal understanding of public relations remains the widespread negative connotations surrounding the term and the tendency for those working in the field of public relations, particularly at senior level, to opt for a range of other titles to describe what they do. While this trend seems unlikely to change, what we can do in this book is to make clear how public relations can and should be understood, what tactics and practices can be deployed, and how PR can be used to help ensure that organisations and their planned activities are better understood and supported by key stakeholder groups and relevant institutions. Of course, to realise its full potential, public relations needs the buy-in and support of senior management to enable it to make strategic, ethical, and coordinated contributions to the objectives the organisation is trying to achieve.

References and additional reading

Bernays, E.L. (1947). The engineering of consent. *Annals off the American Academy of Political and Social Sciences*, *250*(1), 113–120.

Christopher, M., Payne, A. and Ballantyne, D. (1991). *Relationship marketing*. Oxford: Butterworth -Heinemann.

Cohen, H. (2011). *31 public relations definitions*. [Accessed on 17 February 2024] heidicohen.com/public-relations-definitions/.

Grunig, J.E. (2006). Furnishing the edifice: Ongoing research on public relations as a strategic management function. *Journal of Public Relations Research*, *18*(2), 151–176.

Grunig, J.E., & Grunig, L.A. (1992). Models of public relations and communication, In J.E. Grunig (ed.), *Excellence in public relations and communication management*. Hillsdale, NJ: Lawrence Erlbaum Associates, 285–326.

Grunig, J.E. and Hunt, T. (1984). *Managing public relations*. New York, NY: Holt, Rinehart and Winston.

Leadingham, J.A. and Bruning, S.D. (2000). *Public relations as relationship management*. New York: Routledge.

White, C. and Park, J. (2010). Public perceptions of public relations. *Public Relations Review*, *36*(4), 319–324.

2 Models, role and scope of public relations

Danny Moss

Box 2.1 Essentials summary

Discussion about the different forms of PR practice and the role that PR can play within and on behalf of organisations has been a recurring focus for both academics and professionals over the years. Conceptual models, which are simplified representations of real-world structures, activities, and beliefs, have underpinned an ongoing and contested discussion of how PR is best practised. Grunig and Hunt's original (1984) four models of PR: press agentry, public information, two-way asymmetrical and two-way symmetrical PR approaches, have dominated this area of debate. Lack of evidence to support the claimed superiority/excellence of the two-symmetrical model led to Grunig and Grunig (1992) advancing the idea of a continuum of two-way approaches – extending between asymmetrical and symmetrical practices – a 'mixed motives model' which they argued represents the most effective form of PR to secure strategically important long-term stakeholder relationships. Other frameworks or lenses through which the role of PR can be identified and analysed include the notion of 'buffering and bridging', of 'boundary spanning work', and of identifying the influence of the 'environment context' on the role and scope of the PR function's work.

The purpose of public relations

Having examined the way public relations [PR] can be defined, and how we can briefly describe what PR is in the previous chapter, the logical next step is to explore the purpose and role that PR can perform for an organisation and also what role PR professionals play within the function. Given that PR can mean different things in different contexts, one way of capturing the broad differences in the way different organisations and their PR practitioners approach

DOI: 10.4324/9781003129004-4

and practice PR is in terms of a comparison between what are termed 'models' of public relations.

Models of PR

The term 'model' is widely used in most disciplines to describe a 'simplified representation of reality'; a framework created to help make sense of a structure or process within an organisation, industry, or larger entity. In the case of PR, the models encompass the main purpose and role of PR, patterns of communication, intended outcomes, and principal areas where PR is practised. Perhaps the most well-known and widely cited models of PR are the four models advanced by Grunig and Hunt (1984), which they argued not only represented the increasingly sophisticated way in which PR has been practised over time but also captures the different ways in which PR is practised today in different contexts.

The following four models are discussed further:

- Press agentry/Propaganda
- Public information
- Two-way asymmetrical PR
- Two-way symmetrical PR

The distinguishing characteristics of each of these four models are summarised in Figure 2.1a. So, in the case of the press agentry/ propaganda model, practitioners will tend to be focused on persuasion-seeking activities/messages designed to shape the opinions and behaviours of targeted individuals/

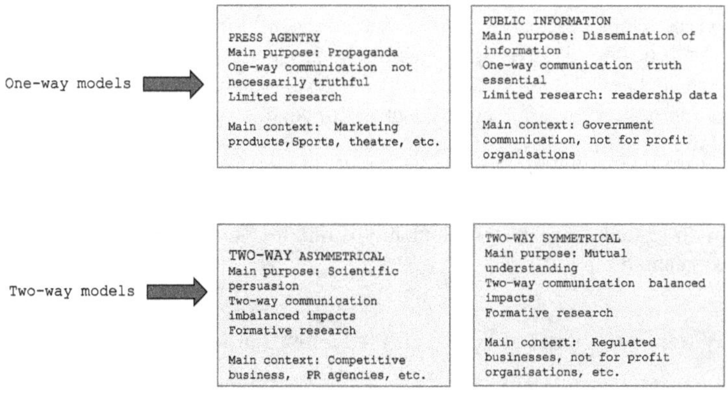

Figure 2.1a Four Models of Public Relations.

Source: Adapted from Grunig and Hunt (1984)

groups. Here, any audience feedback is only used to better refine the persuasive tactics. In contrast, the public information model while still essentially a one-way dissemination model focuses on the accuracy and truthfulness of the information conveyed as a key concern and priority. This type of approach is most closely associated with public health campaigns and other government information campaigns.

With the two two-way models, the distinction between the two models can be seen in their respective purposes. With *asymmetrical* approaches focused on '*scientific persuasion*', where PR activity is directed towards bending or shaping the target public's behaviour in ways that suit or benefit the organisation. The *symmetrical* approach focuses on developing '*mutual understanding*', where the aim is to try to find a balance between the organisation and the target public's interests to achieve a degree of mutual understanding that will allow both parties to reach some form of 'accommodation' in terms of their respective interests.

Of course, the weakness of all models is that they cannot fully replicate what is often a quite complex, nuanced, and sometimes dynamic environment and set of circumstances. This logically may demand that organisations adapt their strategy and pivot as circumstances dictate. Similarly, it follows that the communication/PR approach and strategy would also have to adapt to the scenarios encountered.

In most FMCG companies, for example, the mindset and focus are normally on building product/brand awareness, sales, and market share. It follows that the communication will normally take a predominantly two-way asymmetrical form, seeking to attract and persuade as many potential customers as possible to purchase or order the organisation's products/services. However, in some circumstances, the same FMCG company may have to pivot and change to a more symmetrical format when dealing with special interest groups, employee representatives and regulators, for example, following a serious health and safety issue affecting its products.

With Public Health bodies, much of their communication is about disseminating up-to-date information about health conditions and their prevention. However, during the recent MMR vaccine controversy, health authorities recognised the need to engage closely with opinion leaders/influencers to explain and overcome irrational fears about the side effects of the vaccine so as to try to restore vaccine-based immunity within the vulnerable sections of the population.

Which is the most effective and 'excellent' model?

Before leaving the discussion of communication/PR models, we need to touch on one if not perhaps the central controversy surrounding these conceptual models; namely which, if any, represents the most effective way to practise PR. To some extent, as argued earlier, no one model may be suited to all organisations

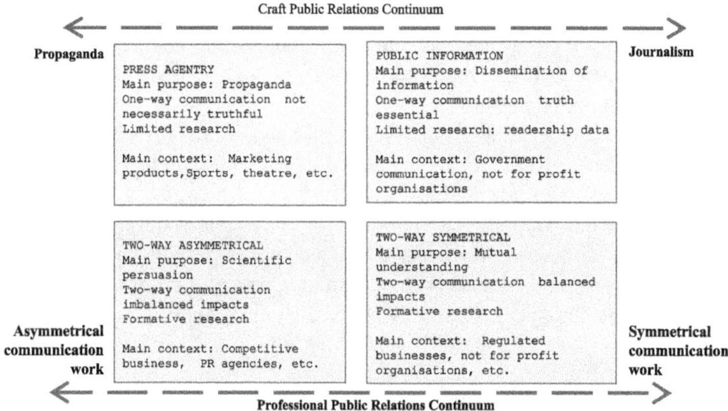

Figure 2.1b The Four Models of Public Relations Positioned on Professional and Craft PR Practice Continua.

Source: Adapted from Grunig and Grunig (1992)

in all circumstances. Nevertheless, Grunig et al. (1992, 2002), in an extensive body of research to uncover what might be termed 'best practice' or 'excellence in PR and communication management', argued that a central feature of excellently managed PR departments was the adoption of the two-way symmetrical approach in managing relationships with the organisation's stakeholders. Reacting to criticism about the idealised nature of this theoretical model, Grung and Grinig (1992) advanced what they termed *mixed motives model* comprising a continuum between two-way symmetrical and two-way asymmetrical practices, which allowed for organisations operating with 'mixed motives' including persuasion and managerial biases. This two-way mixed motives model they labelled 'professional public relations', contrasting this adapted two-way model with a continuum of one-way communication models/practises, which they termed 'craft public relations' (see Figure 2.1b).

Summarising the arguments about models of PR practice

Controversy continues to surround the arguments about the superiority of the two-way symmetrical model/approach, even in its modified form, not the least because of the often-transient nature of organisations deemed to be 'excellently managed'. The arguments can be summarised as follows:

- From the evidence of real-world practices, it seems clear that models at best can only capture in broad and simplified ways how PR might be practised in different scenarios and in different organisational and societal contexts, which may change for each organisation over time.

- This criticism aside, models do offer a useful simplified view of approaches to PR practice that can assist students and new recruits to PR to appreciate how communication practices might impact organisation–stakeholder relationships.
- At the stakeholder relationship level, the notion of a two-way asymmetrical-symmetrical, 'mixed motive' model appears to represent the most realistic reflection of 'best practice'.
- However, the notion of two continua of PR practices (professional and craft PR) has been widely criticised for the implied belittling of craft skills which many professionals point out often represent a set of highly tuned and valued competencies usually honed over many years.

Other ways to understand the role of PR

While this debate about what constitutes the most effective model of PR has dominated much of the academic literature since the early 1980s, these models are not the only 'lens' through which to view and understand the practice of PR and the role it plays for organisations.

Bridging or buffering

One of the most common ways of thinking about the role of PR function in organisations is in terms of a '*buffering role*', performing activities designed to protect the organisation from change or opposition. Here, communication is used to help create and reinforce the organisation's image and reputation. In contrast, some organisations treat PR as fulfilling a '*bridging role*' using communication to reach out and build links with stakeholders in their environment and thereby establish positive relationships with key stakeholders. Box 2.2 provides a brief example of this buffering and bridging role in action.

Boundary spanning role

The notion of PR fulfilling a 'boundary spanning' role is integral in many ways to the idea of PR operating as a two-way symmetrical function and equally underpins the notion of PR as a bridging and buffering activity. The notion of boundary spanners (Aldrich & Herker 1977) is embedded in thinking about how organisations monitor and collect information about their environments to inform management decision-making. Because of the ongoing interaction with organisational stakeholders and the need to continually 'take the temperature' of public opinions about an organisation, PR departments are well-placed to enact this boundary spanning role, albeit working alongside or in conjunction with other outward-facing functions, such as marketing and management information systems (MIS) that also rely on data collection from the external environment.

Box 2.2 Buffering and bridging in action: the Volkswagon emissions case

Prior to the so-called 'dieselgate' crisis, Volkswagon [VW] was one of the most well-known and respected brands on the world stage with annual revenues of over $240 billion. The VW emissions scandal is a well-documented crisis for VW that threatened to severely damage, if not destroy, the company's reputation for reliability and sound engineering, as well as costing the company over $30 billion in fines and compensation payouts around the world to date. The scandal broke in 2015 after VW was forced to admit that it had modified over 11 million diesel vehicles to cheat on government emissions tests. Almost immediately, the then-CEO resigned along with a number of other senior executives leaving the remaining senior management team to 'face the music' of huge fines, multiple lawsuits, and compensation claims. VW's response was to admit to the failings under the previous senior management and pledged to cooperate with the investigation into what had taken place, and to fix the issue as soon as possible. Ongoing communication was to be maintained with all VW customers affected during the period of compensation claims. VW acknowledged that it faced a long road ahead to rebuild trust in the brand's reputation. In 2016, VW began a programme to restore customer trust through initiatives offering customers two $500 free gift cards but this initiative actually sparked an angry reaction in many quarters as a totally inadequate response. Eventually, VW agreed on a compensation settlement firstly with the US government for $10 billion, which offered affected VW owners in the US a buy back or fix for all affected vehicles. This settlement was subsequently rolled out to other affected countries. Throughout the crisis, VW's CC team were clearly fighting a 'rear guard' action attempting to 'buffer' the company from the worse excesses of external criticism, while also reaching out [bridging] to customers and other key stakeholder groups to begin the long process of restoring credibility in the VW brand.

For a fuller insight into the VW emissions scandal, see Tidwell, M (2023).

Multiple operating environments

So far we have explored a number of models and frameworks that can aid our understanding of the broad role, approach taken, and scope of the PR function's work, ranging from PR's propaganda/press agentry role to its symmetrical, relationship-building role, and contrasting PR's buffering and bridging activity, along with its boundary spanning capabilities. A further way to grasp the potentially wide-ranging scope of PR activity is by identifying the different 'environments' in which PR may be called on to operate, each of which contains specific sets of stakeholders and associated issues that tend to be derived from each specific environment. Indeed, environments themselves can be defined in many different ways depending on the criteria used to define their parameters. So, for example, one approach might be to define environments by industry sector – chemicals, manufacturing, mining, retailing, etc. Another approach might be to define environments by market sector – consumer goods or services, industrial goods, transportation, healthcare, etc. Also, multiple criteria could be applied where necessary to help narrow down the targeted section of the population; for example, using socio- or geo-demographics overlayed on a broader market/sector segment. This type of multi-layered targeting is widely used in marketing to help develop specific marketing campaigns for different identified market segments. Moreover, many larger businesses, in particular, may define their markets as international or global, adding a further tier of complication in handling stakeholder communication and relationships across international and even global boundaries.

Figure 2.2 outlines how this notion of the different operating environments is used to indicate the potential scope and breadth of the role and work that PR might undertake for different organisations and in different contexts. The forces and issues arising in any one of these environments are often not entirely compartmentalised and may 'spill over' into other environments,

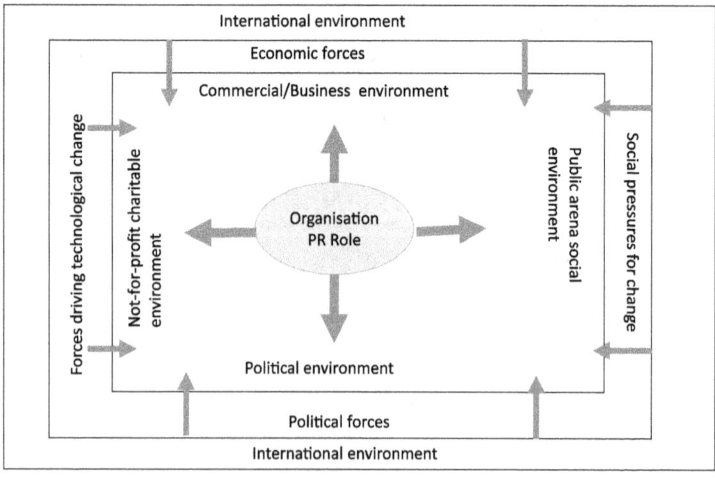

Figure 2.2 The Potential Operating Environments and Forces Shaping the Role of PR.

making organisational responses more complicated and challenging. Thus, for example, the advent of AI technology has potentially huge implications for many industrial sectors around the world, ranging from the creative industries to manufacturing and medicine, with knock-on implications for other forces including economics and work patterns and the demand for labour.

References and additional reading

Aldrich, H. and Herker, D. (1977). Boundary spanning roles an organisational structure. *Academy of Management Review*, *2*, 217–230.

Grunig, J.E. (2006). Furnishing the edifice: Ongoing research on public relations as a strategic management function. *Journal of Public Relations Research*, *18*(2), 151–176.

Grunig, J.E. and Grunig, L.A. (1992). Models of public relations and communications. In Grunig, J.E. (ed.), *Excellence in public relations and communications management*. Mahwah, NJ: Lawrence Erlbaum.

Grunig, L.A. Grung, J.E. and Dozier, D.M. (2002). *Excellent public relations and effective organizations.* Mahwah, NJ: Lawrence Erlbaum Associates.

Grunig, J.E. and Hunt, T. (1984). *Managing public relations*. New York: Holt Rheihart Winston.

Tidwell, M. (2023). The Volkswagon Dieselgate crisis. In Moss, D.A. and DeSanto, B. (eds.), *Public relations cases: International perspectives*. London: Routledge.

3 Public relations practitioner roles

Danny Moss

Box 3.1 Essentials summary

The notion of public relations practitioners performing or enacting various roles, each of which is defined by a particular pattern of activity and behaviour, is fundamental to understanding contemporary public relations practice. In both theory and practice, two dominant practitioner role forms have emerged, namely the *public relations technician role* and the *public relations manager role*. While seen as representing distinctive opposites [often referred to as the manager-technician *dichotomy*], in reality, most practitioners perform or enact elements of both roles – for example, planning and directing a major campaign but also perhaps helping to write material for the media and/or organise events. While the tangible outputs and artefacts of communication produced by technicians are reasonably well-understood, considerable controversy and uncertainty surround the role and work of PR managers – *what PR managers actually do* and *what skills they need to do the job*. Discussion of practitioner roles has become increasingly tied to an examination of the knowledge, skills, personal attributes and work-related competencies associated with each role, and the specific setting or context in which roles are enacted. A recurring issue affecting the public relations 'industry' across the world has been the controversy surrounding the lack of female representation at the manager level – often characterised as the 'glass ceiling' effect. A very similar issue relates to the lack of ethnic minority representation within the industry as a whole. Such concerns raise some important ethical and sustainability issues that the profession has to address going forward.

Defining practitioner roles

The previous two chapters examined public relations (PR) at the functional or department level – how PR is defined, its purpose, and its contribution

DOI: 10.4324/9781003129004-5

to an organisation and to the wider society. In this chapter, the focus shifts to explore the work performed by individual practitioners within their departments or on behalf of organisations, which is generally defined in terms of the particular 'role(s)' that practitioners enact or perform. These roles, in turn, are defined in terms of the dominant patterns of activity associated with each role. While thinking about practitioner roles has continued to evolve since the early pioneering work of Broom (1982) and Dozier (1984, Dozier & Broom 1995), the distinction they drew between two dominant role forms – namely the public relations *technician role* and the public relations *manager role* – continues to shape thinking about the work of public relations practitioners today. What is often referred to as '*manager-technician role dichotomy*' might seem to represent two distinct roles and associated patterns of work, but, in reality, most practitioners tend to engage in elements of both technical and managerial work at different times and circumstances, and particularly so within small departments or agencies where staff numbers may dictate a sharing of all work responsibilities. This said, one dominant role pattern will normally emerge for each practitioner – that is, they fulfil either a predominantly technician or manager role (e.g. see DeSanto & Moss, 2004).

The PR technician's role

The PR technician's role and associated work are generally well understood and well documented, focusing around the creation or production of tangible communication outputs/artefacts including:

- The writing and production of traditional written materials – press releases, brochures, newsletters, reports, visual images, and video material
- Increasingly, the writing and production of content for social media and digital communication channels – tweets, blogs and other social media content
- The production or commissioning of visual materials – photography, video and graphic materials, for stunts, exhibitions, roadshows, etc.
- The organising and implementation of events, exhibitions, stunts, etc.

One notable trend in recent years has been the rapid growth and even reliance on the use of social media channels to reach out and engage with a wide array of target stakeholder groups. However, despite the ever greater reliance on social media channels, the importance and need for the underlying writing skills and high quality visual material has not changed. Indeed, if anything, the demand for such material is all the greater to achieve the 'cut-through' in an ever more crowded media world. Further discussion about these core writing and visual communication skills can be found later in this book.

The PR manager's role

While the PR technician's role appears to be reasonably well understood, far more uncertainty and controversy surround our understanding of the *manager's role in public relations:* what PR managers do and what skills, competencies, and capabilities public relations managers need to demonstrate. The problem here can be traced in part to the way the public relations manager's role has been defined, as well as how the organisation's senior management team understands the PR function.

Early thinking about practitioner roles (e.g. Dozier 1984; Broom & Dozier 1986; Dozier & Broom 1995) attempted to capture the dominant patterns of practitioner work, which they conceptualised in terms of four separate but related role typologies: *public relations technician, communication facilitator, expert prescriber, and problem-solving process facilitators* (see Figure 3.1). However, recognising the need to simplify and strengthen the explanatory value of this framework, the authors went on to collapse these four role models to form the now-familiar dual-role typology comprising: '*the public relations technician*' and '*public relations manager*' roles. Thus, conceptually, the public relations manager role comprised the elements of *communication facilitation, expert prescription*, and *problem-solving facilitation*, which was seen as distinct both conceptually and practically from those practitioners engaged predominantly in devising and implementing tactical

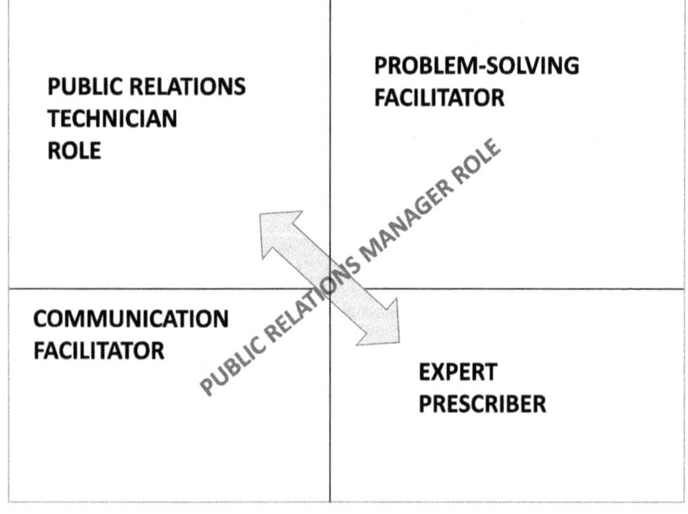

Figure 3.1 Composite View of the PR Practitioner's Manager-Technician Roles.

Source: Adapted from Dozier and Broom (1995). PR Manager-Technician Dichotomy. The two-way arrow infers the interaction between Technician and Manager roles

communication activities. Thus, in short, the public relations manager's role was seen as fulfilling a more complex set of role responsibilities comprising:

- Helping to set up and maintain effective communication channels/networks between an organisation and its relevant stakeholders
- Working as an expert advisor to senior management developing communication-related solutions to identified problems and/or opportunities
- Working more closely with senior management to devise solutions to more complex problems/challenges affecting the organisation's key stakeholder relationships and future success.

Of course, practitioners and PR students today might well criticise this conceptual framework as far too abstract and detached from their experience of the reality of contemporary practice. In particular, the explanation of the public relations manager's role offers only a limited insight into what [public relations] *management work* involves; portraying it as chiefly focused around the planning and implementing of public relations programmes and campaigns. Arguably, what is missing is any sense of the *more strategic tasks and activities* normally associated with senior management as well as the *more routine tasks and activities* normally associated with managerial responsibility – namely, organising, directing, and controlling the rest of the public relations team [where such a team exists], or responsibility for developing strategic plans that are integrated with the wider organisational goals and strategies. In short, the public relations manager's role seems to have been defined in the absence of any reference to the mainstream management theory or literature about the nature of managerial work. What the traditional manager-technician roles framework does recognise is that most public relations practitioners will tend to find themselves working in relatively small departments or teams where there is limited scope for the total separation of manager and technical roles, and hence the reality is that practitioners have to be willing and capable of enacting a *composite role* comprising elements of both *technical and managerial work.*

Practitioner knowledge, skills, personal attributes, and competencies

If understanding the notion of practitioner roles can seem at times quite challenging and abstract, it is often further complicated by attempts to identify and categorise the *associated knowledge, skills, personal attributes, and competencies* required of those professionals engaged at the technician and manager levels. One immediate problem encountered in any such discussion centres on the confusion surrounding the terminology used – distinguishing between *knowledge, skills, personal attributes, and competencies,* which often seem to overlap or even be treated as almost synonymous. While it is beyond the scope of this book to be drawn into a more extensive academic discussion about the relationship between these terms, a basic definition of each of these terms can be found in Table 3.1 which also reinforces the core idea that it is the combining and integrating of knowledge, skills, and personal attributes that enables practitioners to demonstrate specific and relevant core competencies that are critical to performing their job roles effectively.

Finally, before leaving this discussion of public relations practitioner knowledge, skills, personal attributes, and competencies, it might be useful to summarise an inventory of these variables. Here, Tench and Moreno (2015) synthesised the research from a number of studies and from professional bodies to create a useful summary of the range of knowledge, skills, and personal attributes relevant to the performance of public relations roles (see Table 3.2). As noted earlier, it is specific combinations of knowledge, skills, and personal attributes that build into relevant role competencies, and in turn, it is how particular sets of competencies are performed that is central to effective practitioner role performance.

Further insights into the identification of particular sets of role competencies and how they may differ from role to role as well as across different organisational contexts or cultures can be found in the additional reading referenced at the end of the chapter.

Table 3.1 Defining Practitioner Skills, Knowledge, Personal Attributes, and Competencies

Skills are perhaps best defined as those things that practitioners are able to do to perform their job/role effectively. Clearly, the required skill set will tend to depend on the type of job and expertise level at which it is to be performed. As with any particular field, there tend to be some 'core skills' that are fundamental to work within that field – for example, writing skills are almost universal to all the public relations/communication work.

Knowledge is what practitioners need to know in order to perform their role effectively. One of the key issues here is defining the scope of the knowledge needed to perform the public relations role as it might conceivably extend beyond core communication theories and practice and might include scientific understanding, product knowledge, law and ethics, etc. Arguably, the effective public relations practitioner needs to be something of a polymath capable of understanding his/her organisation's business, industry, and the forces shaping the industry's future.

Personal attributes are often thought of as the 'soft/employability skills' – they are separate from competencies, but determine how well a competency is performed. Here, personal attributes include the ability to work in a team, analytical skills, professional experience in a subject area, and general educational level.

Competencies are best thought of as the sets of behaviours that the practitioner can perform – they are based on the application and integration of knowledge and skills in specific contexts. Gregory defines competencies as 'behavioural repertoires or sets of behaviours that support the attainment of organizational objectives' (2008, p. 216). In other words, competencies can be understood as how knowledge and skills are used by individuals to achieve their role objectives.

Table 3.2 Inventory of Practitioner Skills, Knowledge, and Personal Attributes

Skills	*Knowledge*	*Personal attributes*
Writing and oral communication	Business knowledge/literacy	Handling pressure
Project planning and management	Current awareness	Leadership
Critical thinking	Theoretical knowledge	Integrity/honesty
Media skills	PR history	Ethical values
Crisis management	Knowledge of other cultures	Listening
Research	Knowledge of communication models	Confidence/Ambition
Reading Comprehension	Knowledge of how to apply PR theory	Team player
Community relations		Energy/motivation
Consumer relations		Discipline
Employee relations		Intelligence
Professional service skills		Ability to get on with others
Social responsibility		Interpersonal skills
PR ethics/Ethical behaviour		Intellectual curiosity
		Creativity
		Flexibility
		Judgement and decision-making
		Time management
		Respect for hierarchy
		Honesty
		Adaptability
		Willingness to accept assignments
		Finisher completer

Source: Adapted from Tench, R. and Moreno, A. (2015). Mapping communication management competencies for European practitioner. ECOPSI an EU Study. Journal of Communication Management, 19(11)

Management perspectives

While academic research points to how the capability of practitioners to demonstrate role competencies will determine the effectiveness of role performance (Gregory 2008; Tench & Moreno 2015), it is equally important to acknowledge that effectiveness is not always an objective construct, but depends on the expectations and perceptions of senior management. As research over many decades has revealed, public relations is often not understood or fully appreciated as a strategically important function by senior management. A weakness and issue for public relations can be seen in the function's position and reporting relationship within the organisational hierarchy where it reports into. Here, a quite mixed picture seems to emerge, with public relations often reporting into other functions notably marketing or HR rather than having a 'seat at the top table' of its own.

This debate about the standing of the public relations within the overall organisation management structure arguably is also heavily bound up with debates about gender discrimination and the so-called 'glass ceiling' effect on female practitioner advancement.

Gender and practitioner roles

Indeed no discussion of practitioner roles can be complete without acknowledging the persistent issue of gender discrimination. The strong female bias in terms of the balance of male to female practitioners working in public relations is a worldwide phenomenon with various estimates suggesting over 70% of those working in public relations roles are female. However, despite this feminisation of the profession, female gender discrimination in terms of career advancement, status, and salaries has been a constant theme explored within the literature (e.g. See Hon et al., 1992; Toth & Grunig 1993; Aldoory & Toth 2002). Indeed, despite a steady improvement in the recognition of the role of women in the workplace across all sectors over the past 20–30 years in particular, female practitioners have continued to be over-represented within technician roles, and have continued to encounter a variety of obstacles in seeking career advancement – a phenomenon often referred to as the so-called 'glass ceiling' effect.

A number of frequently related obstacles to female practitioner career advancement have been identified over the years, including:

- Institutionalised male prejudice about the capability of female practitioners
- Women have consistently faced exclusion from informal and formal male networks
- Traditional family role expectations on women
- Lack of female confidence and low career expectations in terms of advancement
- Women have not necessarily been less ambitious but have been stifled by the work environment/culture
- Culturally embedded prejudices against women pursuing work-based careers
- Some women self-select to be technicians and have lower career expectations

Perversely, studies across the past four decades have also recorded that women have not always supported other women in progressing their careers. This has ranged from women actively sabotaging their ascent to the power struggles in all-female work environments (e.g. see Yeomans 2019).

While lacking the detailed feminist research into female gender discrimination in public relations, anecdotal evidence strongly suggests that those entering public relations from ethnic minority backgrounds have encountered similar barriers to career advancement as those experienced by female practitioners, particularly within the Western developed economies.

Typical work patterns

Figures 3.2 and 3.3 outline a summary of what a typical 'Day in the Life' of a PR technician and PR manager might look like. These two profiles have been constructed from interviews conducted as part of a research project which was intended to explore the work patterns of experienced PR practitioners. The obvious caveat in reviewing these work patterns is to acknowledge that PR work can often be so highly varied and often quite reactive and hence the notion of a '*typical* day in the life of' can be seen as almost an anomaly.

A day in the life of a PR 'technician'

Julie has worked as a PR Media Officer for XXX, a large energy utility company for three years having joined XXX from a leading regional newspaper in 2019. Julie's key responsibility is to monitor and review the key regional and national news media and social media platforms for coverage of any relevant industry issues/topics and specifically any coverage of XXX bringing any such items to a daily media briefing session with her line manager and three other colleagues at which any immediate responses are discussed and agreed. Here, it is important to note that this work pattern relates to the pre-Covid-19 period and more recent interviews reveal how all of this work had moved to being conducted on a remote basis during the height of the Covid-19 pandemic and has only recently begun to return to a mixed mode of part office and part remote working.

Figure 3.2 A Day in the Life of a PR 'Technician'.

Typical day

Time	Activity
8.30 am	Complete review of national and regional news media and social media platforms – reading through media monitoring and analysis reports submitted by an external media monitoring agency employed by XXX to help with this task
9.15 am	Meet with colleagues and head of department to review media coverage and any other pressing issues and also review individual work plans for the day/week
10 am	Liaise with colleagues on the agreed response to priority issues. Divide up media contact list for one-to-one calls to key contacts

(*Continued*)

Figure 3.2 (Continued)

Time	Activity
10.15-13.30	Call media contacts explaining XXX's stance on key issue while also working on draft media releases to be approved at mid-afternoon team meeting [working lunch at desk]
14.00	Meet with external design agency to review draft designs and materials for a mobile display to be used as part of schools education programme demonstrating the company's work on energy conservation to help address climate change issues
14.45	Reconvened team meeting for update on outcomes of media briefing work. Agree where further effort needed to 'sell-in' XXX's story line and identify opportunities to get XXX spokesperson on media
15.10-16.30	Immediate follow-up to team meeting - redrafting media materials and further follow up contacts with media contacts
16.45-17.30	Meet with HOD to review day's outcome and agree way forward. Also briefing for following evening's hospitality event being part sponsored and hosted by XXX for a large regional children's charity
17.30-18.15	Complete drafting speaking notes for HOD for following evening's charity event and email over to HOD for review
18.30	Leave office with case full of briefing materials to review on journey home

A day in the life of a senior PR manager

Mike has worked in communication/PR for over 12 years first with a large regional local government department and latter with an international consumer goods company based in the company's European HQ in London. Mike's particular expertise and responsibility have been for dealing with regulatory issues and affairs affecting the company's food and household products divisions both pre- and now post-Brexit. As indicated earlier, this work pattern relates to the pre-Covid-19 period, and during the Covid-19 pandemic almost all of the work had moved to being conducted on a remote basis and has only recently begun to return to a mixed mode of part office and part remote working.

Figure 3.3 A Day in the Life of a Senior PR Manager.

Typical day

Time	Activity
8.00 am	Arrive in office having reviewed summaries of all key media coverage relating to the company and its key markets that are emailed to him on a daily basis by the company's media monitoring agency. Identify any key issues needing action ahead of morning communication team meeting. Check any incoming memos/business briefings from senior management team that might have been circulated overnight/early morning

(Continued)

Figure 3.3 (Continued)

Time	Activity
9 am	Communication/PR team meeting for updates on all ongoing action plans and new issues that might need to be addressed
9.45 am	Meeting with senior divisional executives to brief them of about progress with agreed communication strategies and plans and discuss any new issues that have arisen
10.15	Accompany Consumer Business Divisional Head and his team to morning meeting of business sector leaders and Government Ministers at the IoD to launch a new sector initiative aimed at reducing packaging waste and litter
13.30	Meeting back at London HQ office with HR team to discuss recruitment to the communication team
14.30	Catch-up with email and correspondence
15.30	Catch-up meeting with the company's Head of Public Affairs for Europe to review recent developments and future plans
16.30	Cascade meeting with own team to disseminate outcomes of meeting with HOD for PA as well as outcomes of meeting with HR about recruitment. Agree on work plans for rest of the week due to travel to a meeting with communication heads for the company's businesses in the rest of Europe in Madrid the following day
17.30	Re-check email and any outstanding messages before departing office

References and additional reading

Aldoory, L. and Toth, E.L. (2002). Gender discrepancies in a gendered profession: A developing theory for public relations. *Journal of Public Relations Research, 14*(2), 103–126.

Broom, G.M. (1982). A comparison of sex roles in public relations. *Public Relations Review, 8*(3), 17–22.

Broom, G.M. and Dozier, D.M. (1986). Advancement for public relations role models. *Public Relations Review, 7*(1), 37–56.

DeSanto, B. and Moss, D.A. (2004). Rediscovering what PR managers do: Rethinking the measurement of managerial behavior in the public relations context. *Journal of Communication Management, 19*(November), 179–196.

Dozier, D.M. (1984). Program evaluation and roles of practitioners. *Public Relations Review, 10*(Summer 1984), 13–21.

Dozier, D.M. and Broom, G.M. (1995). Evolution of the manager role in public relations practice. *Journal of Public Relations Research, 7*(Spring), 3–26.

Gregory, A. (2008). Competencies of senior communication practitioners in the UK an initial study. *PublicRelations Review, 34*, 215–223.

Hon, L.C., Grunig, L.A. and Dozier, D.M. (1992). Women in public relations: Problems and opportunities. In J.E. Grunig (Ed). *Excellence in public relations and communication management.* Hillsdale NJ: Lawrence Erlbaum Associates.

Sha, B.-L. (2011). 2010 Practice analysis: Professional competencies and work categories in public relations today. *Public Relations Review*, *37*, 187–196.

Tench, R. and Moreno, A. (2015). Mapping communication management competencies for European practitioner. ECOPSI an EU study. *Journal of Communication Management*, *19*(11), 39–61.

Toth, E.L. and Grunig, L.A. (1993). The missing story of women in public relations. *Journal of Public Relations Research*, *5*(Fall), 153–175.

Toth, E.L., Serini, S.A., Donald, K., Wright, D.K. and Emig, A.G. (1998). Trends in public relations roles: 1990–1995. *Public Relations Review*, *24*(Summer), 145–163.

Yeomans, L. (2019). Is a 'new feminist visibility' emerging in the UK PR industry? Senior women's discourse and performativity within the neoliberal PR firm. *Public Relations Inquiry*, *8*(2).

4 Public relations and communications strategy

Danny Moss

Box 4.1 Essentials summary

Despite the widespread use of terms such as public relations or communication strategy in both academic and professional circles, the concept of the strategy remains ambiguous and is often applied inappropriately to describe what, in reality, seems little more than tactical exercises. A better understanding of PR/communication strategy is possible when set against the broader body of corporate and business strategy literature and practice. Indeed, a cursory review of how the concepts of strategy, strategic decision-making, and strategic management have been treated within the PR literature reveals a shameful lack of insight into how thinking has evolved even in the last two decades. So much of the thinking about PR/communication strategy is wedded to a traditional linear planning perspective of strategy and strategic decision-making, ignoring more adaptive, incremental, and interpretive models of strategy (Mintzberg & Waters 1985; Chaffee 1985). The chapter explores several strategies and strategic management frameworks that have emerged within the PR/communication literature and builds an understanding of their strengths and weaknesses. The chapter concludes with a brief examination of Moss and DeSanto's (2011) CMACIE model, exploring to what extent it addresses the notable weaknesses identified in many of the contemporary PR strategy models.

Defining strategy

A broad consensus exists within the business and academic communities that the term strategy is one of the most commonly used but, at the same time, misunderstood concepts in either the communication or general business world. All companies have some form of strategy, if only to guide the direction in

DOI: 10.4324/9781003129004-6

which they are moving. Equally, individual organisational functions such as human resources, marketing, and public relations also need a strategy which arguably links closely to that of the organisation as a whole. But what is a strategy? What does a strategy look like? Who devises strategies? How does communication strategy fit in with other organisational strategies? These are just some frequently posed questions that make it difficult to pinpoint a single universal understanding of strategy.

Strategy hierarchy

Strategy is a hierarchical function which cascades down from the organisational level – 'organisational strategy', which provides the direction and vision of where the organisation as a whole is going, to functional strategies, which determine how the various functions of the organisation contribute to that overall organisational strategic mission and strategy. So, for example, there might be a marketing strategy, as well as human resources, financial management, and, of course, communication/PR strategy. Given that functional strategies draw on and contribute to the overall organisation's [management] strategy, it is logical to start by examining some of the more commonly cited definitions of strategy, which are summarised in Box 4.2.

Box 4.2 Definitions of strategy

Henry Mintzberg, one of the foremost thinkers and scholars on strategy, suggests that strategy is best understood by examining it from a number of interrelated perspectives. He advances his 5Ps framework strategy – Plan, Ploy, Pattern, Position, and Perspective. These five perspectives or approaches, when combined and integrated, offer a more holistic insight into how companies can develop more successful strategies.

Management guru **Peter Drucker (1994)** defines strategy as 'a pattern of activities that seek to achieve the organisation's objectives and adapt its scope, resources and operations to environmental changes in the long term'.

Strategy scholars, **Johnson, Scholes, and Whittington (2006)** define strategy as 'the direction and scope of an organisation over the long term: which achieves advantage for the organisation through its configuration of resources within a challenging environment, to meet the needs of markets and to fulfil stakeholder expectations.'

Mintzberg's 5Ps of strategy

Henry Mintzberg introduced the 5Ps strategy (1987) model as a comprehensive framework for crafting winning strategies (see Table 4.1). This model provides a holistic approach to strategic management, emphasising the importance of considering multiple dimensions in developing effective strategies. So, for example, Mintzberg suggests strategy as both a *position* and *perspective* can be compatible with strategy as a *plan* and/or *pattern*, and management's vision or *perspective* may emerge from previous *patterns* of experience and may lead to the formulation of specific *plans* designed to realise or sustain an organisation's *position*.

One of Mintzberg's (1994) most important contributions to the strategy debate is his emphasis on distinguishing between *strategic planning* and *strategic thinking*. The former, he argues, '*is about analysis whereas the latter is about synthesis*'. In short, Mintzberg argues that strategic thinking creates the vision and ideas that underpin any strategy, and strategic planning helps translate those ideas into a concrete programme of actions/activities to help realise the strategic vision.

Mintzberg also makes an important observation that not all or even most strategies may be *preconceived or pre-planned*, and not all planned strategies may turn out as intended as organisations adapt and change their plans in response to changes in the environment faced. In this sense, the 'realised strategy' may sometimes emerge, only incrementally, as organisations seek to adapt to the circumstances encountered (Mintzberg & Waters 1985).

Although this discussion has drawn heavily on Mintzberg's work, he is not the only management scholar to have written extensively about the concept of strategy. While exploring this broader range of strategy literature might be interesting, it is simply beyond the scope of this chapter to do so in any meaningful way. Nevertheless, we have sought to capture and summarise a number of the most well-known and valuable strategy frameworks in Table 4.2.

Table 4.1 Mintzberg's 5Ps of Strategy

Strategy type/label	*Summary descriptor*
Plan	A predetermined, logical course of action, implementation, and evaluation
Position	An attempt to locate an organisation within its environment/ markets
Perspective	A collective and engraved view of the external world and the organisation's position within it
Ploy	A scheme or manoeuvre designed to outwit opponents
Pattern	A stream of actions that represent a consistent pattern of behaviour

Table 4.2 Summary of Key Concepts, Frameworks, Schools of Thought about Management Strategy

Authors	*Date*	*Summary of key concepts/framework*	*Implications/observations*
Mintzberg, H	1987	Five Ps of strategy – 5 elements – Plan, Ploy, Position, Perspective, Pattern	Strategy may take and combine/integrate different forms and is best understood when viewed through multiple 'lens'
Mintzberg, H and Waters	1985	Notion of intended/planned and emergent/realised strategy	Need for flexibility and adaptability in strategy-making and implementation
Mintzberg, H, Ahlstrand, B, and Lampel, J	1998	Identifies ten different schools of strategy which extend the earlier 5Ps framework: Design school, Planning school, Positioning school, Entrepreneurial school, Cognitive school, Learning school, Power school, Cultural school, Environmental school, and Configurational School	Recognises the multiple and complex nature of how the concept and process of strategy-making is understood. Many of these schools differ largely in their emphasis and may overlap and can be interrelated as was identified with the 5Ps framework
DeWitt and Meyer	2004	The breadth and complexity of strategy-making best captured through a three-dimensional perspective comprising strategy *Process, Content, and Context*	Offers insights into how strategy is made/formulated, who is involved and how decisions are taken and actions implemented and controlled. Emphasises that the content of the strategy will be shaped by the industry and environment context in which the organisation operates

(*Continued*)

Table 4.2 (Continued)

Authors	*Date*	*Summary of key concepts/framework*	*Implications/observations*
Chaffee, E	1985	Suggests three clusters of strategy definitions that differ in their assumptions and processes: Linear strategy, Adaptive strategy, and Interpretive strategy Linear strategy: Rational sequential planning approach Adaptive strategy: Emphasises linking strategy to environment forces and change Interpretive strategy: Stakeholder-oriented strategy seeks to shape/influence stakeholders and gain their support/goodwill	Identifies three hierarchical and increasingly complex and sophisticated perspectives/models of strategy-making. Recognises that no one model can fully explain the nuances and sophistication in approaches to strategy-making used by organisations across differing circumstances
Johnson, G, Scholes, K, and Whittingham	2008	Emphasises the need to recognise and integrate the different levels of strategy – corporate, business, and operational levels of strategy. Highlights the importance of aligning an organisation's internal capabilities with external opportunities and threats as a route to robust sustainable competitive strategies.	Offers useful integrating framework for strategy development at all three levels. Emphasises the 'outside in' and 'inside out' approach to strategy formation along with the importance of responding to stakeholder expectations

For those readers wishing to extend their knowledge of management thinking about strategy, you might find it helpful to refer to another book in the Absolute Essentials series – Witcher, B.J (2020) *Absolute Essentials of Strategic Management.*

Public relations and communications strategy

A recurring criticism of much of the discussion of PR/communication strategy found within both academic and professional works is a failure to draw a clear distinction between *what strategy is* and *what strategy does* (its role and purpose), which becomes all the more important when considering later *how* strategy is formulated.

Just as management strategy should offer a clear vision and guidance for the 'direction of travel' for the organisation/ business as a whole, so PR/ communication strategy should spell out the *purpose, form, focus, and direction* of the communications strategy – how it will contribute to achieving the organisation's overall and specific goals. Creatively, this might be a unifying 'big idea' that will run through and help integrate all communications activities. In addressing organisational issues, the communication strategy statement should indicate the way the communications function will address and respond to the *issues* that the organisation faces, whether these issues are at the corporate, business, or functional levels.

Defining PR/communication strategy

Reviewing the growing range of literature focused on the topic of PR/ communication strategy, a number of essential *themes* can be distilled that help to explain the distinguishing features of 'strategy' in this context:

- Communication strategy defines the *purpose* and direction for the organisation's communications activities.
- Communication strategy helps to *position* the organisation within the environment/markets in which it operates.
- Communication strategy may be expressed as a *plan* or will contain *planned* programmes of communication activities.
- Communication strategy will reflect and give expression to the prevailing management *perspective* of the organisation – the prevailing 'worldview' of the organisation and its position.
- Communication strategy defines the *deployment* of resources across the communication function.

Bearing these themes in mind, it may be helpful to examine some of the conceptual frameworks and models of PR/communication strategy that have been advanced over the years within the academic and professional literature.

Race

One of the oldest and most well-known such models is the RACE framework, which has been utilised as a broad PR planning model/framework since the 1960s. RACE stands for ***Research, Action Planning, Communication, and Evaluation,*** representing the key components that form the foundation of most successful communication campaigns (see Figure 4.1). Essentially, the RACE framework represents a rational, logical, and linear approach to developing an appropriate PR/communication strategy for any given scenario. As such, it equates to Mintzberg's 'planning' perspective and hence has all the acknowledged strengths and weaknesses of this model. The strengths and weaknesses of the RACE model are summarised in Table 4.3.

Given the frequent complexities found in today's business landscape, organisations need to strike a balance between linear planning models and more flexible and adaptive strategies.

By combining the strengths of linear planning models with the flexibility and responsiveness of more adaptive approaches, organisations can create a more dynamic and resilient strategic planning process that is better equipped to deal with uncertainty, change, and complexity.

A dominant planning perspective

Over the years, there have been many emulations of the RACE model although to a large degree most embrace those core elements of analysis, communication

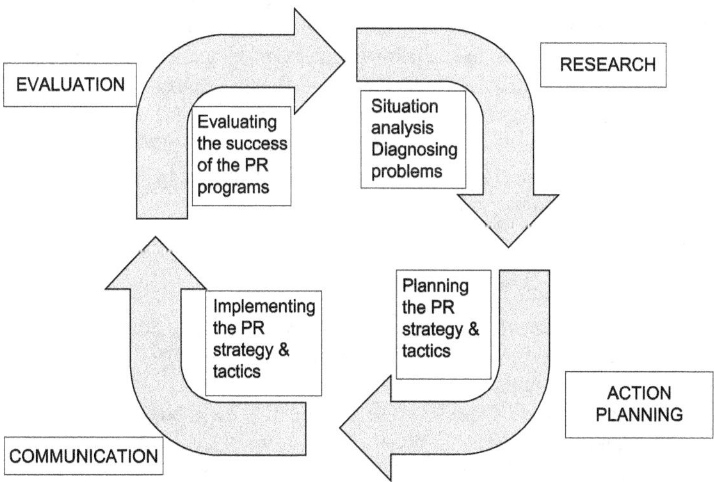

Figure 4.1 RACE Model.

Table 4.3 Strengths and Weaknesses of RACE Model

Strengths	*Weaknesses*
Offers a structured and systematic approach to strategic decision-making	Relies on access to all relevant information at planning stage and little provision for change
A relatively straightforward and logical sequential approach for team members to follow	Lack of flexibility in adaptation. These models are based on the assumption of a linear relationship between inputs and outputs, which may not always hold true in complex and dynamic business environments
Clearly defined lines of accountability and resource allocation	Liable to oversimplify the complexities of the real world. Unsuited to dealing with environments that are characterised by uncertainty, ambiguity, and non-linearity, making it challenging to apply a linear planning model effectively
Plans can be communicated more easily across team members	

planning, implementation, and evaluation. One of the most widely cited and influential studies of PR and communication management – the so-called 'Excellence study' – advanced a seven-stage strategic management model for PR (see Figure 4.2), which if probed 'below the surface' embraces the key elements of the RACE model. In fact, discussion of the PR/communication strategy and strategic management found within both professional and academic literatures has been dominated by the strategic planning perspective. As such, they sit firmly in what Mintzberg would have termed the design school, namely based on the belief that strategy-making essentially involves a logical, *sequential planning process.* While this view seems likely to resonate with most professionals' thinking and direct experience of PR/communication strategy-making, but does raise questions about how the same organisations attempt to formulate effective communication strategies in highly volatile, fast-changing, and uncertain situations.

Strategic thinking and strategic planning

If we accept that *strategic thinking* and *strategic planning* are not the same thing and require different mindsets and skills (Mintzberg 1994), then this distinction is equally important in understanding the process of communication strategy-making. Here, there is still something of a 'black box' when it comes to understanding how organisational visions or big ideas come about – is it through inspiration or perspiration? Similarly, for communication, where and how do the core creative ideas come from that the communication strategies are normally built around?

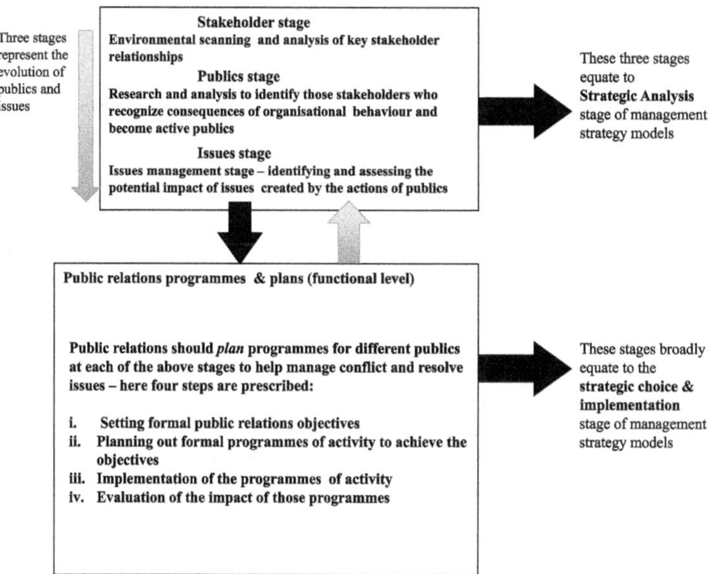

Figure 4.2 Grunig and Repper's Seven-Stage Strategic Planning Model.

Source: Grunig, J. and Repper, F. (1992). Strategic management, publics, and issues in JE Grunig(ed) Excellence in public relations and communication management. Hillsdale, NJ: Lawrence Erlbaum

The 'DNA' of communication strategy

The *strategic thinking* component of the communications strategy-making process can be seen to focus on two critical components of the strategy. First, determining and articulating the *role* that the communications/public relations strategy can or should play in addressing the issues and problems or opportunities the organisation faces; second, determining a *core unifying idea or proposition* that can permeate all the organisation's communications activities. This latter component can be likened to creating the '*DNA*' *of the communications strategy.*

An example of how this DNA analogy can be understood might be where the challenge is to help unite two merging divisions or companies, and explain the new merged entity to the external world. The communications challenge is to tease out those core values that will resonate with and unite the staff within the two merging entities and capture and communicate those values meaningfully to the outside world. Here, the 'communications DNA' is essentially the way those core values are captured and wrapped up in a succinct, communicable message.

Extending this DNA analogy, the core idea should serve as a sort of 'genetic blueprint' – a *recipe* that informs the design of all the components of the communications strategy, which may also extend to all the organisation's communicative behaviours and not just communications through traditional media channels. The communications plan can then be considered a form of 'DNA sequencing', providing the structure and control over the component elements or strategic activities. Of course, not all situations and communication challenges involve complex 'DNA blueprints', or at least, as professionals build up their experience of handling a variety of communication scenarios, they are likely to accumulate a mental bank of tried and tested 'DNA communication blueprint' solutions that can be 'dusted down', and adapted relatively to quickly address the specific situation faced.

Organisations whose communications strategy could be seen to be based around a powerful core idea – a 'genetic blueprint' – that resonates through all their communications as a unique corporate DNA signature include iconic companies such as in the technology sector, Apple; in the automotive sector, BMW, Rolls Royce, or Porsche; in food and retail sectors, McDonald's, Harrods, or Nike; and in transportation and other leisure areas, the Virgin Group. It is not just a case of significant corporates deploying a large advertising budget to help them generate powerful brand recognition. All of these and similarly successful companies have developed a strong core set of values and associated communications propositions – a powerful communications DNA that drives not just their advertising but all elements of their communications strategies.

So, what have we established about PR/communication strategy? Well, it should not be treated as some 'bolt-on' to the organisation's corporate and business strategies; instead, it needs to be closely integrated with those higher-level strategies. Equally, it should not be called on as a corporate 'sticking plaster' to try to combat negative publicity when something has gone badly wrong. To be most effective, an organisation's PR/communication strategy needs to be recognised as important as HR, Finance, Marketing, or any other functional strategy, if not more so, since it may be responsible for how important stakeholders perceive and respond to the organisation as a whole. So, the PR/communication strategy needs to be managed in a highly systematic and accountable manner that ensures that all communication is aligned with and fully supports the corporate vision and direction with the aim of securing and sustaining maximum stakeholder support.

CMACIE communications framework

In looking for a framework to help explain how PR/communication strategy is formulated and managed effectively, what is needed is more than just a logical but limited *campaign planning model*, even though, as we have highlighted earlier, the planning perspective of communication strategy-making continues to dominate professional thinking and experience.

In an attempt to address this weakness in thinking about PR strategy, Moss and DeSanto developed a conceptual framework for PR/communication management that is intended to provide a systematic managerial guide for developing effective organisational PR/communication strategies. This framework draws on both PR/communication as well as management thinking, and also draws on the authors' experience and observation of senior communications practitioner practices across a range of organisational contexts. This framework is based on what management scholars have broadly recognised as the four principal stages or elements that are essential to any complete strategy-making process and also form the key challenges and decision points for the strategic communication management team. These are *situation analysis, strategic choice, implementation and evaluation,* which can be seen to align broadly with the RACE framework that was discussed earlier in the chapter.

Taking this core strategy-making process framework as our base model and adding a 'C' – for communication to each of the four stages allows us to create an easily memorable and relevant acronym – '[C]MACIE':

- Communication Management Analysis
- Communication Management Choice
- Communication Management Implementation
- Communication Management Evaluation

These four stages/elements in the communication management process are elaborated further in Figure 4.3 and arguably encompass the essential decisions and actions communication managers will focus on in formulating the

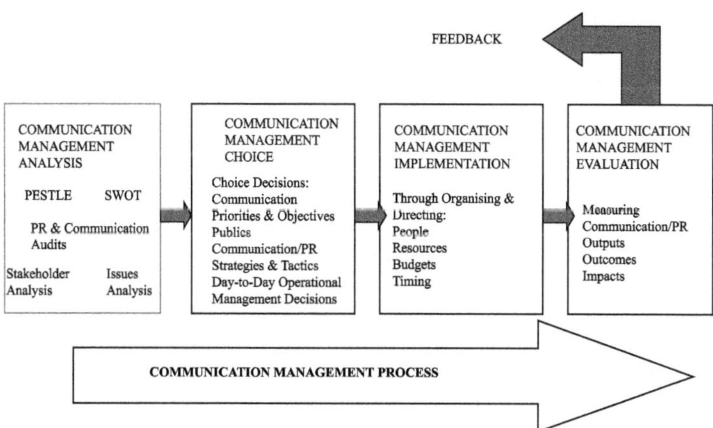

Figure 4.3 CMACIE Model for the Strategic Management of Public Relations.

Source: Moss, D.A. and DeSanto, B. (2011). *Public relations: A managerial perspective*. London: Sage

PR/communication strategy. In some cases, the scenario may dictate the need for an extensive 'multifront' campaign requiring carefully crafted messages and a multichannel delivery strategy. On the other hand, many scenarios might require only a fairly routinised communication response, and as a result, the communication strategy and plans can be agreed upon and managed out relatively straightforwardly.

Not just a planning framework

In drawing heavily on the core management strategy-making framework outlined earlier, it is hardly surprising to find a reasonably close correspondence between the CMACIE framework and most other strategic *planning* models. However, the CMACIE framework differs from other strategic planning models, in at least two important ways: firstly, in terms of its broader focus and explicit intent to focus attention on analysing and interpreting the *management activity* involved at each stage of the process of formulating and implementing strategic communication programmes; second, while on the surface this CMACIE framework might appear to display all the characteristics of strategic planning model, and can indeed be used for that purpose, it is also intended to serve as a more flexible 'skeleton' framework that can accommodate more flexible, incrementally developed communication strategies that may be needed and suited to the more volatile and fast-changing operating environments that many organisations face today.

Turning to the first of these differences, the CMACIE framework is intended to encourage academic and professional interest in analysing and understanding the intellectual and creative processes that lie behind the specific message strategy and combination of PR/communication activities/media that form the core parts of adopted communication strategy. Here, the aim will also be to identify the skills and capabilities displayed by the individuals responsible for the strategy. This reflective analysis is a key element of the CMACIE framework that marks it out from other PR/communication strategy models.

A second distinguishing feature of the CMACIE framework is its ability to accommodate more flexible, incrementally developed communication strategies where volatile market circumstances dictate a high degree of agility is needed. Indeed even back in 2006, Cutlip et al. (2006) acknowledged a growing move towards an '*evolutionary mode*' of strategy formation in which '*strategies may develop over time, representing a pattern of decisions that respond to the opportunities and threats in the environment*' (p 310).

What is essential to acknowledge, however, is the importance of the communications team's analytical skills in capturing the relevant data and making sense of what that data reveals about the situation the organisation in question faces, the issues affecting it, and the impacts on critical stakeholder relationships. The key point is that this analysis should inform the critical *strategic choice and implementation decisions* that determine the shape and ultimate success of the PR/communication strategy adopted.

PR/communication evaluation

Finally, the CMACIE model emphasises the critical importance of the assessment and *evaluation* of the effectiveness of the adopted communication strategy-making process and outcomes. Here, the challenge is to collect and analyse the relevant data that can offer insights into how the component elements of the strategy performed and what obstacles were encountered and how these were overcome. Evaluation is often treated as the *Achilles heel* of the PR/communication industry because of the difficulty of isolating and demonstrating how specific campaigns may have impacted the targeted stakeholder behaviours. However, this is no excuse for not investing in measures to try to track and assess stakeholder responses to communication strategies, utilising the resulting data to better inform future PR/communication strategic decision-making.

References and additional reading

Chaffee, E.E. (1985). Three modes of strategy. *Academy of Management Review, 10*(1), 89–98.

Cutlip, S.M, Center, A, H, and Broom, G.M. (2006). *Effective public relations.* Upper Saddle River NJ: Pearson, Prentice Hall.

De Witt, R. and Meyer, R. (2004). *Strategy process,content, context* (3rd ed.). London: Thompson Learning.

Grunig, J. and Repper, F. (1992). Strategic management, publics and issues. In Grunig, J.E. (ed.), *Excellence in public relations and communication management*. Hillsdale, NJ: Lawrence Erlbaum.

Johnson, G., Scholes, K. and Fuck Whittington, R. (2008). *Exploring corporate strategy*. Harlow: Prentice Hall.

Mintzberg, H. (1987). The strategy concept: Five Ps for strategy. *California Management Review, 30*, 11–24.

Mintzberg, H. (1994). The rise and fall of strategic planning. *Harvard Business Review*, (January–February), 107–114.

Mintzberg, H., & Waters, J.A. (1985). Of strategies, deliberate and emergent. *Strategic Management Journal, 6*, 257–272.

Mintzberg, H., Ahlstrand, B. and Lampel, J. (1998). *Strategy Safari*. New York: Free Press.

Moss, D.A. and DeSanto, B. (2011). *Public relations: A managerial perspective*. London: Sage.

5 Public relations ethics and professional standards

Melanie Powell

Box 5.1 Essentials summary

Ethics at its simplest is the study of right and wrong, and more specifically the study of moral principles and how these ideas are applied to the practice of a particular profession. In Public Relations, professional bodies such as the CIPR and PRCA in the UK provide Codes of Practice applying these principles to set out professional standards. Whilst useful, these Codes have limitations which means it is essential for all PR practitioners to have a basic understanding of key ethical principles and perspectives so that they can recognise and address the ethical issues they encounter in PR practice. This is important because of the power held by communicators, the central role of ethics in reputation and trust, and the conflicting duties of PR practitioners. Key applications in PR practice are ethics in media relations and campaign planning and making ethical decisions. Individual knowledge of ethical principles plus guidance from academic and professional experts can improve ethical decision-making and behaviour for PR practitioners and therefore for their clients and employers.

What are ethics?

Ethics is a big topic: 'the study of what is morally right and what is not' (Cambridge Dictionary (online)). A more specific textbook definition expands this: 'ethics. . . means the formal study and codification of moral principles into systematic frameworks so that decisions can be made about what is right and wrong in a reasoned and structured way' (Gregory 2009: 276).

DOI: 10.4324/9781003129004-7

Some dictionary definitions of ethics go further in linking it with practice in a particular profession: the Cambridge Dictionary further defines ethics as 'a system of *accepted beliefs that control behaviour*, especially such a system based on morals'. What we as individuals, a profession, or a society believe and agree about moral principles determines our ideas of the right/wrong or good/bad ways to practice in a particular expert area such as Public Relations. This is where the concept of ethics meets that of professional standards.

In the UK, professional bodies such as the Chartered Institute of Public Relations and Public Relations Consultants Association have agreed on these principles and made them available in codes of practice (the CIPR Code of Conduct and the PRCA's Professional Charter, 2019). What these have in common is a focus on integrity, honesty, accuracy of information, duty of competence, transparency, and handling conflicts of interest. Both codes place particular emphasis on honesty and truthfulness.

Codes of Practice are useful as they provide guidelines for practitioners and set standards for professional practice which can provide a defence against client/employer pressures to act unethically. Their limitations however are that they tend to be defensive and geared to steering practitioners out of trouble to protect their reputation and the profession's. More importantly, they cannot cover all eventualities. What if you are the first person to encounter a new problem, which often happens in PR because of the ethical implications of new communication technologies?

This is why individual PR practitioners need to know the principles of ethics and how to apply them for themselves.

Ethics is a complex subject. You could dedicate a lifetime to studying it and many people do. This brief introductory chapter can do no more than offer you a starting point, and you are strongly recommended to use the key sources in the Recommended Reading to gain a deeper understanding.

Key ethical theories and perspectives

At its simplest, ethics deal with principles of right and wrong. These principles have evolved over time and people have had very different views of these, based on principles such as religious or philosophical beliefs.

Table 5.1 summarises the key ethical theories and Perspectives which still shape ethical thinking today, with key Personalities, Principles, Places (where we find them today), Problems or limitations, and Pointers (useful tests or points to take away) for each one:

Table 5.1 Overview of Ethical Perspectives (6Ps)

Perspectives *Ethical theory or system of thought*	*People* *Key theorists and dates*	*Principles* *Key ideas*	*Places* *Where we see it today*	*Problems* *Limitations in this view*	*Pointers* *Useful tests or takeaways*
Virtue Ethics	Aristotle (384–322 BC)	Virtue = good 'What would a virtuous man do?' The Golden Mean – moral virtue seeks a middle path	Current views of what is good: Legal system Codes of Practice	The idea of virtue is relative to place and time: we also need values which are universal	Light of Day test: 'What would an ordinary sensible person think?' 'The Golden Mean' – seeking a wise compromise between extremes
Duty Ethics (Deontology)	Immanuel Kant (1724–1804)	Things are right only if done for reasons of duty or principle motives matter. 'Respect of Persons' – individuals matter. Truthfulness Fairness	Human Rights	Truth is an absolute duty – but how does this translate into reality?	Universalisability test: 'What if everyone did that all the time?' Reciprocity or the Golden Rule: 'Do as you would be done by' or 'Treat others as you would want to be treated yourself'
Utilitarian Ethics	Jeremy Bentham (1748–1832)	'The greatest happiness of the greatest number'. Results matter	Democracy Welfare systems Win-win solutions	Rights of minorities within democracy	Useful test: evaluate the results What were the results? How widespread were the benefits?
Discourse Ethics	Jurgen Habermas (1929–)	Discussion and debate are the keys to achieving the right outcomes. A debate set up to be fair and free should have ethical outcomes	Very similar view to dialogue/stakeholder theory, so found in open-systems organisations	In practice, organisations may be reluctant to commit resources to giving their stakeholders a voice	Useful test: 'Are we sure about this?' Fawkes (2021: 275)

Summary

None of these ethical systems is perfect and they do not work in isolation – however, they give us an indication of different ways of assessing good/bad and right/wrong:

Duty ethics – most of the key principles which are important in PR ethics and represented in both the CIPR and PRCA Codes (2019) come from this perspective:

- the idea of **Duty** itself
- **Truth-telling** – a universal duty (a 'must-do at all times')
- **Respect of persons** – informs several other key ideas: Free Will and the freedom to make up your own mind, equality and fairness, being aware of and scrutinising power imbalances, and the Golden Rule.

Virtue ethics – the Light of Day test is a useful quick test of how our thoughts and actions compare with our society's current thinking about what is good/right for an organisation to do – now seen in concepts like CSR and ESG.

Utilitarianism – the idea that results matter and should benefit society as well as the client has clear links with professional communications practice within a democratic system.

Discourse ethics – equal access to communication and problem-solving through dialogue links with the stakeholder and boundary spanning roles of PR and can help organisations struggling with apparently irreconcilable differences with or between stakeholders.

Parsons (2004: 21) summarises key points from these ideas as five ethical pillars or principles to provide a short checklist which is especially useful for making ethical decisions:

Veracity – tell the truth
Non-maleficence – do no harm
Beneficence – do good
Confidentiality – respect privacy
Fairness – be fair and socially responsible.

Practitioner/expert commentator's perspectives

Why are ethics so important in public relations practice?

Two good reasons why ethics are important. First, it's about personal integrity and credibility. Working within an ethical framework such as the CIPR's ethical code of conduct is a mark of any professional. It means that your decisions and actions are explainable and justifiable, and this gives you credibility. It builds your personal reputation as being someone of integrity, and therefore trustworthy. Personal ethics is doing the right thing for the right reasons and it also means being fully competent to practice so you can give the best possible advice.

Second, you will be working for someone in due course. You will be one of their main representatives and part of your job will be to guard your organisation's reputation. Reputations are built on making good, ethical decisions. You will have challenging conversations with senior colleagues if their decisions and actions potentially threaten that reputation. So, you will need to be sure of your ethical ground and be able to argue for it. Similarly, when you talk to people outside the organisation, such as journalists and the local community, you will need convincing arguments for the position it takes. Arguing from an ethical stance makes that a whole lot easier.

Dr. Anne Gregory, Professor Emeritus of Corporate Communication, University of Huddersfield

Ethics is about what you do and how you do it. It concerns choices we make as PR practitioners. So, ethics is important in *doing* good work and *being* a good person. It starts with *knowing* what good means.

This is where codes of conduct are helpful within the profession, as well as for organisations that employ PR and how it is seen in wider society. Codes define the parameters of ethical work and provide guidelines to meet these standards in practice.

Compliance with codes and other regulations is the backbone of ethical practice. It's our public demonstration of responsibility, personally and as a profession. Words like honest, truthful, and accountable translate in practice to commitments, for instance, to fact-checking and transparency in use of AI.

Being a good person involves commitment to professional development. We enhance our ethical judgement, performance, and competence by practising ethical decision-making and reflection.

Our sustainable intention should be to cultivate an Ethics of Care comprising considerate communications and relationships with humans and non-humans (including animals and environments). Such thoughtful practice is important as it's inherently reflexive in how we care about and for others, give and receive care, care with affinity, and seek self-care.

Heather Yaxley, PhD, Managing Consultant, Applause Consultancy

Public relations has a unique position in an organisation, and with the clients we work for. We are often the ones bringing the outside, in. We do the horizon scanning and take the temperature across a range of stakeholders to enable our employers to communicate effectively. If we don't apply good judgement and ethical considerations to that role, then we cannot provide effective support. Working in PR is a privilege because of that, and as someone new to PR, thinking and behaving ethically is as important as the words we write and the plans we develop.

Hayley James Chart, PR, FCIPR,
CIPR Board Director

Summary

Public Relations is about communication, which has the power to change people's knowledge, attitudes, and behaviour and ultimately to bring about social change, with good effects or bad. Hence, the choices made by individual public relations practitioners will shape the society and ultimately the world we live in in the future – and the stakes have never been higher. This applies to all the types of communication used by PR practitioners:

- **Informative communication** – information is a valued commodity, and having or not having it affects the decisions people make about their lives. Having information and being able to decide whether to release or withhold it is an enormous source of power. Having the skills to judge how and when to best communicate it, and the ability to choose whom to include and exclude is a further source of expert power.
- **Persuasive communication** – power is associated with influence, which in PR means the ability to change people's attitudes and behaviour through persuasive communication. This raises the ethical issues of whether this change is achieved fairly and truthfully, with what effects and who benefits.

PR practitioners face difficult decisions with an ethical component every day – balancing conflicting duties and responsibilities to many stakeholders whilst at the cutting edge of difficult issues, whilst under daily public scrutiny. Being aware of ethical principles and how to apply them is vital in this task.

Applying ethics to PR practice

We can now turn to examine how these ethical principles can be applied to Public Relations practice – first to ethical considerations in Media Relations, PR campaign planning and evaluation, making decisions which are difficult because they have an ethical component, and finally to the role of ethics in leadership.

Ethics in media relations

Many new PR practitioners start out in Media Relations: yet this is an area of practice with many complex ethical issues.

Different ethical codes – Both PR professional Codes and those of the National Union of Journalists endorse openness and honesty and the public interest.

However, journalistic codes place more emphasis on the importance of media freedom, a clear division between advertising and editorial coverage, and the concept of 'the public's right to know', often invoked as a defence against allegations of intrusion or libel. As a PR practitioner, your duties of confidentiality and care to your client and/or employer and to vulnerable stakeholders have to be balanced with your duty to the public interest and will normally come first (except if the organisation is doing something so bad you have to consider whistleblowing – in which case you need to seek legal and professional advice as it is an extreme step.)

Power imbalance – The increasing pressures and shrinking resources facing many news media raise the risk of PR practitioners using their power to give or withhold information and access to influence, coerce, or even bully journalists or to come under pressure from employers or clients to do so.

Telling the truth versus 'Spin' – There are many shades of this: selecting only flattering information, stating just the positives not the negatives or 'sexing up' a story – embellishing the truth to create a narrative which fits news values better. And when do agenda setting and framing stop being legitimate benefits of being proactive and shade into spin?

Parsons (2016) suggests four Pillars of Ethical Media Relations to address these issues:

- Honesty and accuracy – this should be equally important to PR practitioners and journalists because of the wider social importance of published information being true.
- Judiciousness – making accurate judgements on the importance of information we send based on news values.
- Responsiveness – *[e.g. 'Endeavour to honour promises and respect deadlines and inform media contacts as soon as possible if there is a problem.' – Media Spamming Charter PRCA, CIPR, IRS (Investor Relations Society), and NUJ (2010)].*
- Respect – Respect of Persons plus showing that you know and respect principles important to them, plus just politeness and consideration!

Ethics in PR planning

PR planning is arguably the activity where the power of the PR practitioner is at its maximum: your employer or client has entrusted you with considerable resources to use communication to achieve the change they are seeking. What you achieve and how you achieve it can either enhance or damage their relationships or reputation.

PR campaign models do not usually show the ethical as well as strategic decisions to be made at each step. Powell (2011) suggests how this may be done for the CMACIE planning model (see Chapter 4) and for the PR planning process in general (see Table 5.2).

Table 5.2 Ethics and Key Steps in the PR Planning Process

PR planning step	*Ethical questions*	*Key ethical perspectives*
Analysis		
Stakeholder analysis	Is a broad *all-stakeholder* perspective being used? Are minority/vulnerable stakeholders included? (Mainstream stakeholder models which prioritise based on power may exclude them)	Utilitarianism – 'Greatest happiness' Duty Ethics – organisations may have a duty of 'Respect of Persons' to these groups which justifies their inclusion
Choice: Communication strategy	Inform, persuade, or involve via dialogue?	All these raise different ethical issues – see Summary (p. 54–55)
Objectives	Do the objectives set have the potential to do good? Who will benefit?	Utilitarianism – results matter. The wider the benefits, the better the results
Implementation: Tactics	Are the tactics truthful, fair, and honest? Do they match the organisation's ethical values? If persuasive, is the persuasion fair or unfair? Is the target audience treated with respect? Are all tactics safe? Has risk management been used to make sure they will not harm any stakeholders?	All of these are from Duty Ethics – Truthfulness Free Will Respect of Persons 'Do no harm' Duty of Care
Evaluation	Did the campaign meet the TARES test for ethical persuasion (Baker and Martinson 2002)? 1. Truthfulness 2. Authenticity 3. Respect for rights of the audience 4. Equity 5. Social responsibility	#1–4 are all from Duty Ethics #5 from Utilitarianism – 'greatest happiness of greatest number'

Ethical decision-making

In PR practice, where conflicting duties must often be considered under time pressure means that PR practitioners are frequently faced with making difficult decisions which have an ethical component.

Working knowledge of ethical principles enables practitioners to apply them in a reasoned and logical way to understand and find a solution to ethical issues, using much the same strategic process that they would use to resolve a PR issue. Many theorists have created step-by-step models for ethical decision-making (the Potter Box (1972); Sims (1992); Trevino and Nelson (1993); Seib and Fitzpatrick (1995), which are usefully analysed, summarised, and updated by Parsons (2004). Table 5.3 shows Parsons' (2004) model related to familiar PR planning steps:

Table 5.3 Ethical Decision-making

PR planning stages plus additional ethics steps	*Ethical decision-making (Parsons 2004)*
Research	1. Gather all relevant information
Analysis	2. Clearly define the problem
Values	3. Identify your professional values – such as truthfulness, doing no harm, doing good, confidentiality, and fairness
Ethics	4. Apply ethical principles – look at it from the point of view of Virtue Ethics, Duty Ethics, Utilitarianism, Discourse Ethics, etc.
Stakeholder/Duty	5. Who are the stakeholders in the situation? What are your duties/loyalties to them?
Strategy	6. Make a decision
Checking*	7. Check it
Action	8. Take action
Documentary	*9. Record your decision (Powell 2011)*

Source: Adapted from Parsons, P.J. (2016). Ethics in Public Relations: A Guide to Best Practice (3rd ed). London Kogan Page

* For step 7, Sims (1992) suggests two quick tests:

- What would my family think?
- What if I read about it in a newspaper?

This framework offers a quick check with your personal ethics (likely to have come from your family) and the news media as a quick method for wider social values (the Light of Day test).

Powell (2011: 419) adds a final step: *record your decision* so that if necessary, you can explain it in an internal or public inquiry or court case to demonstrate that whatever the outcome, you used due professional diligence in arriving at it.

Fawkes (2021) questions how far rational ethical decision-making models fit with reality and individual experience. She suggests instead an approach of heightened self-awareness: discomfort with a decision, power or lack of power to act, and ability (or not) to discuss these feelings (2021:275). Her alternative 'quick check': "check your own inner responses and have the courage to pause and ask those around you: Are we *sure* about this?" uses feelings rather than principles and logic as a guide. Moreover, by initiating dialogue this kickstarts 'Discourse Ethics': arguably the ethical perspective which best fits PR's abilities.

Summary

Ethics is the formal study of moral systems and principles. What we as individuals, a profession, or a society believe and agree about these determines our ideas of the right/wrong or good/bad ways to practice in a particular expert area such as Public Relations.

Professional bodies such as the CIPR and PRCA have agreed on these principles for the PR profession and made them available in the CIPR's Code of Conduct and the PRCA's Professional Charter (2019). These include integrity, honesty, accuracy of information, duty of competence, transparency, and handling conflict of interest.

However, Codes of Practice have limitations, making it important for all PR practitioners to have a knowledge of ethical perspectives such as Virtue Ethics, Duty Ethics, Utilitarianism, and Discourse Ethics so that they can identify and respond to ethical issues independently.

Ethics is important in PR because of the power of communication, its key importance in reputation and trust, and the conflicting duties of the PR practitioner.

To be ethical, informative communication must be truthful and accurate with careful fact-checking; persuasion must be fair and allow people to make up their own minds; and two-way communication must offer stakeholders a fair dialogue.

Key applications of ethics in PR practice are recognising and addressing the ethical issues in media relations and the PR campaign planning process, and making ethical decisions.

Key ethical issues in media relations are the differing ethical values held by PR practitioners and journalists, possible power imbalance between them, and the problem of 'spin'.

Being aware of the key ethical as well as strategic decision points in the PR planning process should help to achieve outcomes which are ethical as well as effective.

Ethical principles can be applied in a logical process to recognise ethical dilemmas and make decisions you feel comfortable with, can explain, and are prepared to stand by.

Finally, ethics is complex but its essence is simple: 1. Do no harm. 2. Do good.

If practitioners were to follow such basic principles and apply this 'litmus test' to their decisions and actions, they would almost certainly avoid some of the difficulties and even crises that can result from decisions and actions that result in serious stakeholder protest and worse, wider public outrage and media condemnation that can prove extremely damaging to any organisation's reputation.

References and additional reading

Bailey, R. (2022). *Briefing:Professional ethics.* 4th April PR Academy [Online] [Accessed on 26 December 2023] https://pracademy.co.uk/insights/briefing-professional-ethics/

CIPR (no date). *Code of conduct.* CIPR [Online] [Accessed on 26 December 2023] https://cipr.co.uk/CIPR/About_Us/Governance_/CIPR_Code_of_Conduct.aspx

CIPR (no date). *Ethics hotline* and *decision tree*, CIPR [Online] [Accessed on 26 December 2023] https://cipr.co.uk/CIPR/CIPR/Our_work/Policy/Ethics.aspx

CIPR (2023). *Everyday ethics in PR case study collection.* CIPR (Members' Area) [Online] [Accessed on 26 December 2023] https://www.cipr.co.uk/CIPR/Membership/Benefits/everyday_ethics_in_pr.aspx

Fawkes, J. (2021) Public relations' professionalism and ethics. In Tench, R. and Waddington, S. (ed.), *Exploring public relations and management communication* (5th ed.). Harlow: Pearson.

Gregory, A. (2009). Ethics and professionalism in public relations. In Tench, R. and Yeomans, L. (ed.), *Exploring public relations* (2nd ed.). Harlow: Pearson.

L'Etang, J. and Pieczka, M. (2006). *Public relations: Critical debates and contemporary practice.* Mahwah, NJ and London: Lawrence Erlbaum Associates.

Parsons, P.J. (2016). *Ethics in public relations: A guide to best practice* (3rd ed.). London: Kogan Page.

Powell, M. (2011). Ethics and the public relations management process. In Moss, D. and DeSanto, B. (ed.), *Public relations: A managerial perspective*. London: Sage.

PRCA (2019). *PRCA professional charter and codes of conduct* [Online] [Accessed on 26 December 2023] https://www.prca.org.uk/about-us/pr-standards/professional-charter-and-codes-conduct

Potter, R. (1972). The logic of argument. In P. Deats (eds.) *Towards a discipline of social ethics.* Boston: Boston University Press.

Seib, P & Fitzpatrick, K. (1995). *Public relation ethics.* Fort Worth Texas: Harcourt Brace.

Sims, R.R. (1992). The challenge of ethical behaviour in organisations. *Journal of Business Ethics, 11.*

Trevino, P. & Nelson, K.A. (1993). *Managing business Ethics*, Chichester, NY: Wiley.

Yaxley, H. (2022). *CIPR applied ethical practice playbooks: 1. Fact-checking; 2. Ethical decision-making; 3. Regulation; 4: Reflective ethical practice.* CIPR (Members' Area) [Online] [Accessed on 26 December 2023] https://www.cipr.co.uk/CIPR/Our_work/Policy/ethical_playbook.aspx

Part 2

PR applications and specialisms

6 Corporate communication

Danny Moss

Box 6.1 Essentials summary

There is considerable confusion and ambiguity over the relationship between corporate communication and public relations – initially in terms of which is the parent discipline. Theoretical relationship between the two disciplines in which corporate communication is essentially a specialist sub-discipline of public relations focused in particular on corporate stakeholders such as shareholders, employees, customers, other industry members, the local community, and perhaps industry regulators, does not necessarily mirror the wider practitioner view in which corporate communication is the most significant strategic function, whereas public relations is treated as primarily a tactical media relations-related function. Corporate communication is typically recognised as a strategic communication function responsible for managing the organisation's key stakeholder relationships and anticipating and managing responses to key issues that may impact the organisation's operations and longer-term reputation.

Introduction: defining corporate communication

In the first chapter of this book, we highlighted the continued ambiguity surrounding our understanding of public relations with the multitude of definitions that exist, merely adding to the degree of confusion surrounding precisely what public relations is. Arguably, we can see a very similar pattern surrounding the understanding of corporate communication (CC), with definitions being advanced from a number of different perspectives. Moreover, this definitional confusion also extends to how the relationship

DOI: 10.4324/9781003129004-9

between CC and public relations (PR) is understood. Perhaps the most popular narrative portrays PR as essentially a technical, creative function focused on the communication/information dissemination between an organisation and its publics (either one-way or two-way), whereas CC is seen as a fully-fledged managerial function that has gradually developed from a more craft-orientated PR function (van Riel 1995; Cornelissen 2004).

From this managerial perspective, CC is responsible for harmonising all internal and external communication as effectively as possible. Moreover, it is also suggested that managerial perspective helps to enable CC professionals and departments to gain greater recognition and status amongst senior management circles within an increasing number of mainstream businesses, where 'corporate communication', corporate affairs, or public affairs departments have become increasingly accepted as part of the mainstream organisational hierarchical structure (Cornelissen 2004). What needs to be acknowledged here is that despite the assumed greater managerial orientation that is claimed to help distinguish CC from public relations, the two share many common features, particularly in terms of the communication tools and practices used. Moreover, no universally accepted definition of CC has emerged; instead, a range of definitions of CC have been advanced that reflect and draw on different disciplinary perspectives. A summary and comparison of some of the more widely cited definitions can be found in Box 6.2.

Box 6.2 Definitions of CC that focus on the idea of CC as a strategic management function

> *Corporate Communication is the orchestration of all the instruments in the field of organisational identity (communications, symbols and behaviours of organizational members) in such an attractive and realistic manner as to create or maintain a positive reputation for groups with which the organisation has an interdependent relationship.*
>
> (van Riel 2003: 53, https://www.emerald.com/insight/content/doi/10.1108/CCIJ-12-2011-0073/full/html#b63)

> *The set of activities involved in managing and orchestrating all internal and external communication aimed at creating favourable starting points with stakeholders on which the company depends. Corporate communication consists of disseminating information*

by various specialists and generalists in an organisation, with the common goal of enhancing the organisation's ability to retain its licence to operate.

(van Riel & Fombrun 2007: 25, https://www.emerald.com/insight/content/doi/10.1108/13563281211274121/full/html#b61)

Definitions that focus on a broader total communication perspective of CC

Corporate communication encompasses and manages all of a company's communication activities as an integrated whole with the aim of building and maintaining a valuable corporate reputation across different stakeholder groups, markets and audiences.

(Christensen & Cornelissen 2011, https://www.emerald.com/insight/content/doi/10.1108/CCIJ-12-2011-0073/full/html#b8; Cornelissen 2008, https://www.emerald.com/insight/content/doi/10.1108/CCIJ-12-2011-0073/full/html#b12)

Definitions where CC is seen to contribute to a broader marketing and integrated marketing communication perspective

Integrated Marketing Communication (IMC) is the process of developing and implementing various forms of persuasive communication programs with customers and prospects over time.

(Kitchen et al. 2004: 22, https://www.emerald.com/insight/content/doi/10.1108/CCIJ-12-2011-0073/full/html#b40)

Here, IMC follows an 'inside-out logic' with all contact points between the company and customers recognised as contributing to the communication impact on organisational reputation and customer loyalty.

One view that captures a number of lines of argument is that CC includes three categories of communication defined by the senders or the receivers of the communication (van Riel 1995):

1. *Management communication* is implemented by senior managers for planning, organising, supervising, coordinating, and monitoring. It is useful to develop a shared vision within the organisation, gain and maintain trust in corporate leadership, enable and manage change processes, and finally, help employees to grow professionally.

2. *Organisational communication* includes heterogeneous communication activities, including public relations, public affairs, CSR communication, investor relations, communication with the labour market, corporate advertising, and internal communications.
3. *Marketing communication* encompasses commercial communication activities developed to support the sale of goods and services. It typically includes the promotional mix: advertising, direct mail, personal sales, and product sponsorship.

Exploring the common features found across a number of the established definitions of corporate communication (van Riel 1995; van Riel 2003; Goodman & Hirsch 2010; Cornelissen 2020), three main themes seem to emerge:

- First, CC is generally recognised as a strategic management function, with its communication activities aligned to the company's overall strategy.
- Second, CC usually seeks to integrate external and internal communication activities across a range of organisational practices to build, maintain, or change positive images and reputations.
- Third, all these activities take place inside relationships with the external and internal stakeholders of the organisation.

Stakeholders for corporate communication

Drawing on the third of these common features, it follows that CC can involve targeting a potentially broad and diverse range of stakeholder targets. However, as with all communication strategies, it is invariably the situational context that dictates not only the communication priorities and options, but the situational analysis will also encompass the identification and prioritisation of the specific stakeholder groups and individuals that each CC campaign strategy will need to target. While this maxim holds true for virtually any communication campaign, CC professionals based in any particular organisation will typically have a set of crucial stakeholder targets whom they will be continually monitoring and analysing in terms of their connection to the organisation and to the issues on their priority monitoring agenda. So, for example, oil and gas exploration companies which operate in a highly politicised, environmentally scrutinised industry need to continually monitor government thinking around potential changes in the already high levels of taxation imposed on the industry, as well as monitoring the intensive scrutiny of health and safety issues at extraction and processing facilities. These issues and their implications for the associated stakeholder groups can be monitored and analysed using a variety of tools, such as an issues–stakeholder matrix (see typical example in Table 6.1).

Table 6.1 Example of a Typical Issues–Stakeholder Matrix

Issues/stakeholders		*Level of taxation*	*Regulatory Licence*	*Health and safety*	*Environment concerns*	*Exploration costs*	*Transportation*
Prioritisation	Ranking	(1)	(2)	(3=)	(3)	(5)	(6)
Employees							
Regulatory authority	(1)						
UK Government	(3=)						
International government bodies	(3=)						
Shareholders/financial institutions	(2)						
Pressure Groups-e.g./Geenpeace	(5)						
Local communities	(6)						
Industry bodies	(7)						
Competitors	(8)						

In which stakeholder can be prioritised against relevant issues, assigning a value to designate the issues likelihood of occurrence and potential strength of impact. By repeatedly updating and testing the accuracy of the predicted issues/stakeholder outcomes, it may be possible to refine the stakeholder analysis and the accuracy of the predicted impact of issues. This analysis will then be fed to the CC strategy planning.

Priorities can be assigned to both issues and various stakeholders either using a numerical scale or on a colour-coding basis. The assigned priorities can also change over time as events unfold. New issues and stakeholders can also be added to the matrix where appropriate. Once completed and then updated, this type of matrix analysis can feed into the planning of the CC strategy.

Each organisation will tend to have a different set of specific stakeholders, reflecting both external and internal considerations that, to a greater or lesser degree, shape the organisation's relationship with its stakeholders. Here, external considerations include the type of industry setting and the economic, political, and technological conditions affecting that industry and the specific organisation. Equally, internal considerations such as internal history, organisational culture, and operating methods and approaches may shape the nature and priorities amongst the potential stakeholder groups. While acknowledging that each organisation and situation will tend to dictate a specific set of stakeholder targets, there will still be a broadly generic set of stakeholder categories that most CC strategies will have been tracking and can then be prioritised or not in any particular scenario. For the majority of organisations, these mainstream CC stakeholder categories include:

- Shareholders and financial institutions (broken down by the significance of their shareholding)
- Institutional investors (where appropriate). Again broken down by the significance of their shareholding
- Employees and trade unions
- Government (relevant departments/ministries)
- International governments (where appropriate)
- Regulators
- Other industry bodies
- Clients and customers
- Suppliers/supply chain members

Issues for corporate communication

The starting point for most organisations in issues monitoring and analysis will tend to be a broad core of potential issues that you might expect to find on the agenda of most corporations, albeit many of these may be monitored relatively passively unless there is some spike of activity that raises the prominence and threat level from that issue's area. These broad issues categories are summarised as follows:

- Government regulation: monitoring government interest and activity in relation to the industry relevance legislation
- Taxation levels: monitoring government interest and indicated policies concerning industry taxation
- Workforce retention/recruitment and skills: Monitoring perceptions of the organisation as an attractive option for talented new recruits and levels of existing employee engagement and satisfaction
- Health and Safety: Site/plant safety measures and protocols are used to monitor H&S training and measures across the organisation's facilities. H&S track record
- Technological change, especially AI: Impact of new technologies and particularly recent AI developments for organisation systems and processes and decision-making
- Supply chain/just in time: Impact on supply chain effectiveness of geopolitical and economic world events
- Economics, especially inflation: ongoing monitoring of economic shifts and trends to anticipate the impact on the organisation's operations and business model

While many of these issues are primarily of relevance and concern to mainstream management in terms of their business and management decisions, there will nevertheless be a communication dimension to each, if only in terms of how the reaction to and resolution of these issues might impact the organisation's core stakeholder relationships and reputation.

Beyond this broad issues monitoring (boundary spanning function), most significant organisations/corporations will tend to identify and track the number of specific core issues that affect their industry/sector over time, translating this ongoing issues analysis into a much more specific set of actionable issues (and associated stakeholders) for any particular scenario that the organisation needs to confront. The significance and even frequency of the issues faced will undoubtedly vary from industry to industry. Some sectors/industries undoubtedly face very specific issues, particularly those that are more heavily regulated, such as financial services, nuclear energy, water and utilities, and mining and oil/gas exploration/processing. This said, organisations need to be prepared to handle whatever challenges and opportunities they encounter. Many of these can be anticipated by ongoing monitoring and analysis of trends and developments across the environments in which they operate or plan to operate.

Corporate communication strategy and implementation

Arguably, CC plays a vital role in the success of any organisation, underpinning the building of strong relationships with internal and external stakeholders that are often essential to achieving business objectives. Effective CC can play a crucial part in conveying the organisation's vision, values, and goals to employees, customers, investors, and the public.

Moreover, because of the constantly accelerating pace of technological change, particularly the huge expansion and influence of social media in recent years, where information spreads rapidly, maintaining a consistent and coherent CC strategy can be vital in protecting the organisation's reputation and corporate image. Corporate image and reputation (see Box 6.3 for more about corporate reputation) are critically important in building trust and credibility among stakeholders, which is essential for long-term success and sustainability.

Box 6.3 Corporate reputation

Because of the increasing exposure to scrutiny and criticism that all organisations can experience due to the expansion of social and digital media and the expectations of greater transparency, an organisation's reputation can play a crucial role in its success and sustainability. Corporate reputation is perhaps best thought of from a stakeholder-centric perspective, encompassing how a company is perceived by its stakeholders, including customers, employees, investors, and the general public. It reflects the organisation's values, actions, and overall impact on society. Reputation influences not only customers' choices but also an organisation's ability to attract and retain talented employees, as well as influencing attitudes and behaviours towards the organisation from most other stakeholder groups/individuals. Organisations can attempt to influence their reputations – ideally seeking to enhance them through well-crafted CC campaigns designed to inform and enhance stakeholder perceptions of the organisation. However, generally, a 'good' reputation has to be earned through consistent policies and behaviours on the part of an organisation over time and cannot be 'manufactured' through some 'glossy' CC campaign. In short, CC can help inform stakeholders about an organisation's values, activities, and impact on its business environment and wider society, but it cannot dictate how stakeholders will respond and think about the organisation. This is where CC might sometimes need to 'hold a mirror up to' senior management to help them see how others perceive the organisation and, hence, what actions they need to undertake to change those perceptions.

As we have pointed out in other chapters of this book (e.g. see Chapter 4), the core elements of communication strategy development are broadly similar across most communication fields/disciplines, ranging from internal communication to marketing communication and public affairs. What makes each disciplinary communication strategy distinctive is not the components of strategy or steps involved in the process of strategy formulation per se, which are broadly common across the areas of PR/communication operation, but the specific content of the component decisions taken in formulating the strategy. So, for example, the type of communication objectives that are set, the message strategies adopted, and perhaps even the type of communication activities utilised, all of which stem from the critical drivers in formulating any communication strategy – namely, the *specific issues identified and the particular stakeholders and stakeholder relationships* that the strategy is intended to impact, both of which were examined earlier.

So, while the core elements of planning and implementing any CC strategy might not, on the surface, differ significantly from those found in other organisational functions, it is worthwhile briefly summarising what these components comprise:

Key components of CC strategy/strategy implementation are as follows:

1. **Situation analysis**: Analysing the industry and environment context – part of the issues analysis process in which CC professional operate in their 'boundary spanning' role, monitoring and prioritising key issues and challenges for the CC strategy.
2. **Stakeholder target public analysis**: Identifying and understanding who needs to be targeted and why so that key messages can be appropriately crafted. Different stakeholders may have varying communication preferences and needs, and tailoring messages to resonate with each group is crucial.
3. **Message development**: Creating clear, concise, and compelling messages is at the core of any communication strategy. The messages must be aligned with the organisation's positioning and goals and easily understood by the intended target audience(s).
4. **Media and activity selection**: Choosing the right communication channels to deliver messages is key to effectively reaching the target audience.

Whether through traditional media, digital platforms, or face-to-face interactions, selecting the appropriate channels can enhance the impact of communication efforts.

5. **Evaluation**: Monitoring the outcome and impact of the CC strategy and tactics implemented, particularly in terms of the resolution of the critical issues identified and the longer-term reputation and positioning of the organisation.

Corporate communication campaign activities

Looking at the range of communication activities or tactics that might be deployed to achieve the intended CC outcomes, again there are many similarities with other areas of PR/communication work. So typically, traditional media and, increasingly, social media relations will normally figure prominently in any campaign strategy, but here, the specific publications or social media outlets will be selected to reach the type of stakeholder audiences being targeted. Other activities such as conference attendance, exhibition work, events, specialist reports, and brochures may all be part of a specific campaign strategy. Table 6.2 provides a broad summary of some of the types of PR activities/tools that CC might call on to reach different stakeholder audiences.

Evaluation of corporate communication

As with most areas of PR/communication, evaluation of CC has proved problematic with far too much reliance on simply analysing media coverage or social media 'likes' or 'hits' achieved, which at best indicates the successful placement of information/stories in the media/social media, not the genuine impact that coverage might have had on those who / saw read it. This emphasis on 'process' measurement has continued over the years, mainly because of the difficulty and cost of measuring communication 'impact' accurately. The problem here is that, in practice, communication does not take place in a sterile laboratory setting; it is often impossible to isolate and measure the impact of communication activity from all the influences/distractions that might shape peoples' thinking and behaviour. To try to do so has proved both challenging and expensive, and so many organisations have turned to buying customised media analysis and social media analysis services that do at least show that there has been some measurable output for the resources expended. What larger organisations can and often do is monitor longer-term perceptions of their reputation amongst stakeholders and perhaps brand perceptions as indicators, albeit indirect indicators, of the effectiveness of their CC activities.

Table 6.2 Corporate PR/Corporate Communication Activities/Tools

Target stakeholder/ publics	*Type of scenarios/issues*	*Typical range of communication activities used- primary*	*Typical range of communication activities used- secondary*	*Assessment Evaluation of success*
Employees and management	Ongoing employee comms Industrial disputes Structural change/ redundancies, etc.	Employee newsletter/e-newsletter Intranet/corporate website Meetings with Mgt	Local media news releases Company website – community pages Local community sponsorship and secondments	Labour turnover ability to fill vacancies Ongoing staff survey about levels of satisfaction with roles as well as pay and conditions
Customers and clients	New product launch Ongoing customer relations Product failure/quality complaints	Launch events/stunts Corporate and brand web pages Media/key customer Site visits and briefings Expert panels and Press briefings to address issues	Ongoing mainstream media, trade media, and social media programmes to maintain profile and brand reputation	Monitoring media/social media coverage Customer feedback via web page and after-sales feedback
Suppliers and intermediaries	Supply chain breakdown Quality issues with components	Website updates Trade media releases Facilitate face-to-face mgt meetings Possible trade show/ exhibition stands	Trade media briefings Updates to company website	Trade press/media monitoring Letters pages, interviews Website feedback Trade show feedback and trade

(*Continued*)

Table 6.2 (Continued)

Target stakeholder/ publics	*Type of scenarios/issues*	*Typical range of communication activities used- primary*	*Typical range of communication activities used- secondary*	*Assessment Evaluation of success*
Investors/ shareholders	Release of trading results Issuing of trading update – good/ bad Adverse share price movements Hostile takeover bid/offer	Facilitate release of results to stock exchange Prepare annual and interim financial reports Financial media briefing Stockbroker plant/HQ tours and briefing with senior mgt	Social media liaison Updates to company website information Briefings for institutional investor teams	Financial market reaction – share price movements, investor responses Financial media coverage and sentiment Direct feedback on company's social media
Local community [LC]	Plant/factory/office closure or opening Impact of production on environment	Facilitate meeting/ briefing by senior mgt with local community representatives Media plant tours/visits Briefing with local councillors and local MPs	Website updates about any planned plant closure plant Updates via X, Facebook, etc.	Local media monitoring Letters pages, interviews Website feedback Social media monitoring
Local government	Link to LC issues Planning applications	Facilitate one-to-one briefing of appropriate MPs by senior mgt	Website updates along with selected social media	Ultimately local government policy changes/action Local/regional media reporting/ sentiment of coverage
Regulators	Imposition of tighter industry regulations Breach of existing regulations – by accident or deliberately	Facilitate meetings and factory visits for regulator officers Prepare documentation for regulator to indicate compliance	Ongoing website updating and content creation including compliance-related information	Regulator reports and feedback plus outcome of any regulatory policy decisions affecting the organisation Website feedback Social media feedback

References and additional reading

Christensen, L.T. and Cornelissen, J. (2011), Bridging corporate and organisational communication: Review, development and a look to the future. *Management Communication Quarterly*, *25*(3), 383–414.

Cornelissen, J. (2004, 2020). *Corporate communications: A guide to theory and practice*. London: Sage.

Kitchen, P.J., Don E. Schultz, D.E. Kim, I., Han, D., and Li, T. (2004). Will agencies ever 'get' (understand) IMC. *European Journal of Marketing*, *38* (11/12).

Goodman, M.B. and Hirsch, P.B. (2010). *Corporate communication*. New York, NY: Peter Lang.

Van Riel, C.B.M. (1995). *Principles of corporate communication*. London: Prentice Hall.

Van Riel, C.B.M. and Fombrun, C. (2007). *Essentials of corporate communication*. New York: Routledge.

7 Public relations and marketing

Danny Moss

Box 7.1 Essentials summary

Marketing and public relations (PR) share some common goals, such as creating awareness and building relationships, but they differ significantly in their approach, breadth of target audiences, and goals. Marketing is focused on identifying and satisfying customer needs and thereby driving sales and profits through persuasive communications and other promotional activities. PR can and does support marketing in terms of its publicity-generating role, but more strategically helps to create a more receptive environment for marketing by building ongoing trust, credibility, and goodwill towards an organisation with a broader range of stakeholders, including the media and diverse publics. Recent changes in consumer media consumption and, notably, the rapid growth of social media platforms have also forced marketing and PR professionals to re-examine their media channel strategies and priorities. Marketing communication and public relations can be important elements of a well-designed integrated marketing communication (IMC) strategy that can help to build a strong brand, drive sales, and enhance an organisation's reputation.

Introduction

One of the most enduring and yet contentious relationships over the years has been that between marketing and public relations (PR) functions. While there is no denying the potential close and supportive relationship between the two functions, there has equally been an ongoing tension and often mistrust between marketing and public relations professionals, particularly in terms of the functional hierarchy, and power and control, centring on the question

DOI: 10.4324/9781003129004-10

of who determines operational policies and tactics. This chapter will not only explore these issues and tensions but also examine how marketing and public relations can complement one another. We also explore the emergence of notions such as 'marketing-PR', examining why the advancement of such notions might threaten to destabilise the relationship between marketing and PR professionals even further.

Defining public relations and marketing

The initial chapters of this book focused on defining public relations and its role in contemporary organisations and society. Here, if necessary, you might re-examine those earlier chapters and revisit the key ideas underpinning how we understand and define public relations. In short, the argument advanced is that PR is most effective when practised as two-way communication process that seeks to build and maintain mutually beneficial understanding and relationships between organisations and their publics (e.g., Grunig & Hunt, 1984; Cutlip et al, 2006); rather than simply directing communication at targeted audiences to try to shape their behaviour. So if we accept that PR is primarily concerned with building relationships with an organisation's relevant stakeholders in order to create and sustain the goodwill needed to enable the organisation to continue to go about building its business, how does it differ from marketing? Before it is possible to examine the relationship between PR and marketing, we first need to establish what marketing is as a professional and business practice, and how it has been defined.

Defining marketing

Marketing is essentially a 'transactional' function focused around the exchange of values; normally products or services in exchange for payment. Of course, for such exchanges to take place effectively and consistently, organisations need to understand what goods and services people wish to buy and, perhaps more fundamentally, what particular needs are those goods and services intended to satisfy. This distinction between products and needs is perhaps best exemplified in the cosmetics industry, where the founder of one well-known brand of cosmetics was claimed to have explained that while cosmetics companies make beauty products, what they are actually selling to customers in the store is 'hope'.

Formal definitions of marketing advanced by the two leading professional bodies for marketing in the UK and the US (see Box 7.2) are very similar in many ways, focusing on marketing as the function responsible for managing the exchange relationship between an organisation and their customers and for identifying and meeting customer needs (profitably).

Box 7.2 Definition of marketing

CIM (The chartered institute of marketing in the UK)

> *Marketing is the management process responsible for identifying, anticipating and satisfying customer requirements profitably.*
>
> (2023)

AMA (American marketing association)

> *Marketing is the activity, set of institutions, and processes for creating, communicating, delivering, and exchanging offerings that have value for customers, clients, partners, and society at large.*
>
> [AMA 2017]

The four and seven P's of marketing

While definitions help to capture and explain the overall role and purpose of marketing, it is perhaps easier to understand what marketing does for an organisation and what marketing decisions focus on by examining the key elements of operational practice. Here, operational decisions and activities are best captured in terms of the well-established 4'Ps' and more recent 7'Ps' framework. The former conceived in the 1960s by McCarthy (McCarthy, 1964) comprised the following core elements:

- **Product**: the physical or intangible offering that a company provides to its customers. Including the design, features, quality, packaging, branding, and any additional services or warranties associated with the product.
- **Price**: refers to what customers are willing to pay for the product or service. The price set not only affects the company's profitability but also influences consumer perception and purchasing decisions.
- **Place** (Distribution): refers to the strategies and channels used to make the product or service accessible to the target market, including the choice of distribution channels, retail locations, online platforms, and logistics.
- **Promotion**: comprises all the activities a company undertakes to promote the value of its product or service to the target audience, including advertising, sales promotions, public relations, social media marketing, and other methods used to create awareness and generate interest amongst the target audiences.

As marketing thinking has extended to consider the growth of emphasis in the provision and sale of services, it was recognised that the traditional marketing mix [4Ps] needed to be adapted to reflect additional key dimensions in the delivery and user experiences of services. As a result, the 4Ps have been expanded to include a further three elements – *people, processes, and physical evidence:*

- **People:** customer-facing staff can play a key part in representing the organisation and in the customer experience and this is particularly critical in the marketing of any service. In the professional, financial, or hospitality service industry, people are the 'products' themselves.
- **Processes**: refers to the set of activities involved in the delivery of the product/service benefits. Processes may comprise those tasks performed by staff that shape customer perceptions/experiences.
- **Physical evidence:** refers to the non-human elements of the service encounter, which might include the equipment used and the facilities in which the product/service is delivered. It may also refer to the environment in which customers encounter products or experience the service including the design of facilities, colour schemes, and layout.

So, having examined some core definitions of marketing and PR as well as their respective dimensions/characteristics, it might be helpful to summarise how the two functions compare across a number of these key dimensions/characteristics. This comparison is set out in Table 7.1.

Marketing and PR's early relationships – friends or adversaries?

Traditionally, and certainly before the more recent rapid expansion of online and digital marketing communication activity, marketing and PR tended to see themselves as adversaries, competing for a larger slice of whatever promotional budget was available. Indeed, the relationship between marketing and PR has always been a somewhat ambiguous and controversial one, at least when considering how the two functions operate in the business/commercial arena. In this commercial context, marketing professionals and academics (e.g. Kotler 1991) have tended to treat PR as the 'inferior partner' in the relationship, with PR playing a predominantly publicity-generating role in support of marketing. In essence, PR being treated as part of the 'promotional element of the 4Ps'. This narrow, essentially asymmetrical view of PR has been most commonly found within the fast-moving consumer goods sector (FMCG), which traditionally has tended to rely on mainstream media advertising (print and TV) campaigns to push their brand and sales

Table 7.1 Comparison of Marketing and PR: Key Distinguishing Characteristics

Distinguishing dimensions/ characteristics	*Public relations*	*Marketing*
Definitions	*Public Relations is about reputation – the result of what you do, what you say and what others say about you. Public Relations is the discipline which looks after reputation, with the aim of earning understanding and support and influencing opinion and behaviour.* Grunig and Hunt (1984) define public relations as *The function responsible for the 'management of communication between an organisation and its publics'.*	*Marketing is the management process responsible for identifying, anticipating and satisfying customer requirements profitably* (2023) AMA (American Marketing Association). *Marketing is the activity, set of institutions, and processes for creating, communicating, delivering, and exchanging offerings that have value for customers, clients, partners, and society at large* [AMA 2017].
Type of goals/outcomes	Stakeholder relationship-building, reputation enhancement, and protection	Sales, Market share, Profit
Key target audiences/publics	All key stakeholders might include consumers and employees, government, etc.	Consumers, end users, intermediaries, influencers
Key relationship outcomes sought	Creating and sustaining the goodwill with stakeholders needed to achieve business goals	Focused on facilitating the exchange of values – goods and services for payment
Strategic and operations decisions	Key publics, messages, communication channels/ activities to reach target publics	Key decisions around 4Ps – Product, price, distribution, and promotional channels tailored to satisfy consumer needs
Form of communication	Both two-way symmetrical and asymmetrical communication	Generally two-way asymmetrical and also at times one-way persuasive/sales-orientated communication
Size of budget	Generally relatively small compared to marketing	Can vary significantly but generally far larger than PR
Position within the senior management structure	Traditionally not part of top management team but reports to members of that team	Increasingly recognised as part of senior management team

messages at identified target markets. In this context, the role of PR typically might include:

- Helping to support and extend the reach of any advertising/promotional campaigns, especially where the promotional budget is under pressure and PR can be used to generate additional media coverage.
- Building credibility for the marketing offer by securing expert reviews and feedback for the product/ service.
- Building awareness and hence credibility for the company through well-targeted media releases, profile pieces, and product news stories.

It is probably true to say that both marketers and PR professionals acknowledge that in the marketing context, PR does normally fulfil a predominantly publicity role – as part of the promotional mix, helping raise awareness of products or services, and brands, and helping move potential customers along the 'sales funnel' to purchase or re-purchase. However, this is not the only role that PR can play in this context. As highlighted earlier in chapters, PR has a broader remit than marketing's customer relationship focus, one that embraces managing an organisation's relationship with all its stakeholders, including customers, employees, investors, and the general public. Here, PR role is essentially focused more broadly on managing this array of stakeholder relationships so as to defend, maintain, and/or strengthen an organisation's reputation (see Chapter 6 for further insights into corporate reputation management). Of course, these marketing and reputation-management-related roles are not incompatible and, indeed, often coexist and complement one another, building and reinforcing consumer confidence in the product/service brand. Indeed, in Chapter 1, we pointed to the CIPR's definition of PR as almost synonymous with the notion of reputation management. An example of how PR's broader reputation management role might be deployed to improve the overall positioning and reputation of an organisation, which can then impact the organisation's commercial success, can be seen in the case of Iceland Foods (see Box 7.3).

Box 7.3 Iceland's palm oil initiative

In an intensely competitive UK food retail sector, Iceland has struggled to maintain its position and market share as a specialist frozen food supplier against a backdrop of ever-growing competition from discounters such as Aldi and Lidl and cost-cutting from the major supermarket chains such as Tesco and Sainsbury. Yet despite these pressures, Iceland under the control of the Walker family ownership has continued to champion a strong environment campaigning stance. Under the current leadership of Richard Walker, Iceland embarked on a series of campaigning initiatives designed to reinforce the company's credibility as a thought leader in the sustainable retailing 'space'. Perhaps the most high profile of these initiatives has been its commitment to supporting the use of only sustainable palm oil and to the reduction of palm oil content within its supply chain. With Richard Walker taking a prominent campaigning lead, Iceland launched a series of initiatives to educate the public and industry about the impact of palm oil deforestation in Borneo in particular. This anti-palm oil campaigning stance culminated in the company's planned Christmas (2018) advertisement and promotional campaign focused around an animated film created by Greenpeace featuring Rang Tang, a baby orangutang that had lost its mother and its forest home due to palm oil harvesting. The advert was ultimately blocked by the regulator because of the political connections with Greenpeace. However, Iceland's PR team and agency [Shandwick] was able to turn this 'banning' of its Christmas advertisement to its advantage, generating extensive media coverage of this decision and arranging media interviews for Richard Walker to explain Iceland's position. The Rang Tan film was released on social media channels where it was viewed over 80 million times across Iceland-owned channels and it sparked 350 million social media conversations. By the end of 2018, Iceland's YouGov Brand Buzz score (a measure of trust, consideration, and perceptions of quality and value) was the highest for a decade. Consumer consideration of Iceland grew to the highest of any retailer, placing Iceland ahead of Waitrose.

For a more detailed insight into the case, see Berg, H. (2023) 'Iceland Foods: Rang Tan and the palm Oil alarm call' in Moss, D, and DeSanto, B (Eds). *Public relations cases: International perspectives.* Routledge

PR's more tactical role

Perhaps the most obvious way in which PR can be deployed to work alongside and, in fact, become seamlessly integrated into marketing strategies is in terms of promotional sales-related campaigns. Indeed, there might well be some questions raised as to whether such activities are, in fact, PR or marketing. Equally, one might question the merits of even trying to make any such distinction – Why should it matter what we label a particular activity provided it works and achieves intended goals? The answer is normally that

of 'territorialism' or organisational power politics. Traditionally, promotional tactics that marketers might deploy could include:

- Large sales discounts – such as 'the Black Friday' or July Sales seasons
- Special price offers – returning customer discounts, Club card/store card loyalty prices
- Discount/money-off coupons – traditionally distributed via magazines or newspapers but now often digitalised and available online or as an e-coupon sent to mobile phones
- Free giveaways – in a variety of forms 2–1 offers, prize draws associated rewards linked to purchases
- Competitions and other rewards – free to enter draws, etc.
- On-pack redemption offers – collect packet tops and redeem them for rewards
- Multipack offerings – bulk pack purchase offers, for example, buy a case of wine for a 25% discount on normal bottle price.
- Product celebrity endorsement – for example, celebrity player endorsement of sports equipment – trainers, golf clubs, or tennis rackets

With the growth of online commerce and retailing, an additional range of promotional activities has come to the fore, which arguably are more readily identifiable as sitting under the PR 'umbrella', although how such activities are designated and managed in practice may vary from organisation to organisation. Examples include:

- **Monitoring and reacting to media inquiries:** represents a mainstream PR media relations tactic of building solid links with mainstream and social media journalists establishing your organisation as expert source of content on relevant subjects
- **Newsjacking:** is another media relations tactic of monitoring opportunities to 'piggyback' on contemporary news stories, responding rapidly and offering expert opinion/commentary on relevant topics
- **Product placement and endorsement:** although regulated to avoid unjustified overuse of product props, this tactic involves the free provision of products or payment to film/TV producers to include specific product brands at appropriate points in a film/TV series – Ray Ban Sunglasses were worn by Tom Cruise in the film *Top Gun*; Aston Martin partnered with EON Productions to provide its iconic sports cars for the James Bond movies.
- **Using brand ambassadors-influencer marketing:** recruitment of influential figures [celebrities or figures with large social media following] as 'brand ambassadors' has become an increasingly important tactic in so many of today's social media-driven marketplaces. A good example of this successful influencer marketing strategy is Heinz's PR campaign with the

famous musician Ed Sheeran, who's a big fan of their ketchup and who has a huge social media following [see **bit.ly/48vnq7q**].

- **Partnering with other brands:** where two brands share values and common traits in their audiences, they may collaborate in special promotions to appeal to both customer bases
- **PR stunts and 'Guerilla' marketing:** PR stunts are anything unusual a company does to create media buzz and generate media coverage. 'Guerilla marketing' campaigns are similar to PR stunts, but guerilla marketing is generally associated with outdoors, low-cost, and even more unconventional and daring activities – for example, Beefeater Gin covered the Oxford Circus Tube station with the signs and smells of strawberries for two weeks to promote the launch of their Strawberry Gin. Absolut Vodka placed battered and open cases containing a bottle of Absolut vodka on the baggage carrousel at Schiphol airport labelled 'Absolut Temptation' which captured the travelling public's attention.
- **Linking the brand values to a cause:** where a company does hold strong convictions about particular issues/causes, there is an opportunity to emphasise this point of difference in its marketing tactics. Patagonia repeatedly emphasises that it cares about the planet and sustainability. It reinforced this message in the advertising message attached to one of its jackets listed on Black Friday '***Don't buy this Jacket***'.

All these tactics have one thing in common; namely the goal of attracting existing or potential customer attention and encouraging them ultimately to move towards purchase or repurchase of the organisation's offering.

Integrated marketing communication (IMC)

The concept of *integrated marketing communication* (IMC) emerged during the late 20th century and has arguably grown in importance with the proliferation of media channels and the fracturing of mass media audiences (e.g. see Kitchen & Burgmann, 2015; Schultz et al, 1993). The term refers to the strategic coordination and integration of the array of available marketing and PR communication channels and tools to deliver a consistent and unified message to the target audience – what is sometimes referred to as creating a seamless brand experience. IMC recognises that consumers may encounter and be exposed to multiple touchpoints and channels, including advertising, public relations, direct marketing, social media, sales promotion, and digital marketing. Traditionally, these various channels would have been treated separately, with specific campaigns designed for each channel. In contrast, under an IMC approach, the aim is to align and weave together the messaging and use of channels to deliver a cohesive 'orchestrated symphony' of communication in one integrated strategy. In short, IMC is seen to offer a highly customer-centric

Box 7.4 Dove # The Selfie Talk campaign

Building on high profile campaigning role in support of body positivity for women, Dove's PR and social media team put together a *#TheSelfieTalk* initiative aimed at young girls and women, to enable more open and positive discussion of how young women perceive and talk about body images.

The campaign included two digital download kits: one for parents and one for teachers. Each kit included ways to talk to kids and teens about selfies and how to embrace individuality and body positivity.

The aim of this PR-led initiative was part of the longer-term strategy to position the Dove brand as a leader in this field of improving female attitudes and thinking about body image. What this case illustrates is how a well-constructed, longer-term, values-based PR campaign can enhance a brand's position and reputation, and thereby enhance its long-term market prospects.

approach that maximises the impact of multiple channel usage and helps ensure consistent brand communication and consequent brand recognition, which should lead to greater brand engagement and brand loyalty.

From a PR perspective, the main question is not whether or not PR should be treated as part of the IMC mix, but rather how the PR element of the mix is best managed. Generally, the PR activity will normally come under the overall direction and control of the senior marketing officer overseeing the IMC campaign, but would be carried out by PR professionals with the necessary professional expertise.

This Dove case illustrates how PR can work collaboratively with mainstream marketing/branding strategies to build credibility and favourability towards an organisation and its brands.

MPR – a source of friction

While not materially affecting the practical application of PR activities to support marketing strategies, the late 1990s saw the controversial emergence of the notion of 'marketing public relations' (MPR). Indeed, MPR was heralded by some commentators as a 'new discipline' comprising the specialist application of public relations techniques to support marketing activities. Here, for example, Harris (1991) claimed 'MPR should be differentiated from' general public relations' and corporate PR. This claim sparked an inevitable counterargument from PR professionals and academics that it amounted to little more than an attempt by marketing professionals and academics to 'hijack' the promotional arm of public relations – a form of 'marketing imperialism' (Kitchen & Moss 1995).

Putting such arguments over power and functional 'labels' aside, what does seem clear is that there has been a marked growth in the use of PR activities to support mainstream marketing strategies as the effectiveness of traditional marketing activities has declined in the face of marked changes in consumer media consumption patterns, in part at least brought about by the expansion in the use of social media. Faced with the challenges of trying to communicate with a more well-educated and more cynical younger consumer, engaging far less often with traditional media channels, it is hardly surprising that marketers have turned to PR and social media to replace some of their more traditional promotional methods to communicate about both the organisation and the products/services.

Summary

This chapter acknowledges the view that marketing and PR should be understood and practised as two distinct but nevertheless interrelated functions. From this perspective, marketing is recognised as focusing on promoting products or services to generate sales and revenue; while PR focuses on managing the reputation and relationships of an organisation with all its stakeholders, including customers, suppliers, employees, investors, and the general public. Working collaboratively rather than adversarially, the two functions can enhance brand reputation, increase customer engagement, and drive business growth.

References and additional reading

Berg, H. (2023). Iceland foods: Rang Tan and the palm Oil alarm call. In Moss, D. and DeSanto, B. (eds.), *Public relations cases: International perspectives*. London: Routledge.

Cutlip, S.M., Center, A.H., and Broom, G.M. (2006). *Effective public relations*. (9th Ed)., Upper Saddle River, NJ: Pearson Education.

Grunig, J.E. & Hunt, T. (1984). *Manging public relations*. New York: Holt, Rinehart, Winston.

Harris, T. (1991). *The market's guide to public relations: How today's companies are using the new PR gain competitive advantage*. New York: John Wiley & Sons.

Kitchen, P.J., and Burgmann, I. (2015). Integrated marketing communication: Making it work at a strategic level. *Journal of Business Strategy, 36*(4), 34–39.

Kitchen, P.J. and Moss, D.A. (1995). Marketing and public relations: The relationship revisited. *Marketing Communications, 1*, 105–119.

Kotler, P. (1991). *Marketing Management. (7th Ed)*, Englewood Cliffs Prentice-Hall.

McCarthy, J.E. (1964). *Basicmarketing: A managerial approach*. Homewood, IL: Irwin.

Schultz, D.E., Tannenbaum, S.I. and Lauterborn, R.F. (1993). *Integrated marketing communications*. Lincolnwood Ill: NTC Business Books.

8 Internal/employee communication

Carl Holloway

Box 8.1 Essentials summary

An organisation's employees are often touted as the organisation's most valuable resources, but are often the last to know about where the organisation is going and why because of inadequate internal communication (IC). Here, effective IC is often seen as key to promoting and maintaining employee 'engagement' – to maintain a highly motivated workforce. A highly engaged workforce is seen as critical in building competitive success in terms of how well employees interface positively with external stakeholders.

The type of challenges that IC is normally concerned with include maintaining management–employee information flows, disseminating organisational goals, strategy and performance across the organisation, helping to motivate employees, assisting HRM in managing relationships with employees and trades unions during industrial disputes, and helping to communicate organisational values and beliefs that underpin a strong culture. Here, IC can deploy a range of traditional and newer digital communication tools to achieve these outcomes. Thus, the status of IC has undoubtedly been elevated in recent years as its role in helping to sustain a more engaged workforce has gained recognition.

Defining internal communication

There are many broadly similar attempts to define Internal Communications (IC) ranging from more theoretical or conceptual definitions such as: 'Internal communication is the sharing of information, knowledge, and ideas within an organization, with the goal of ensuring alignment, engagement, and productivity among employees'; to more process-related, pragmatic definitions such as 'Internal communication is an entire process within an organization. It includes

DOI: 10.4324/9781003129004-11

how information is shared up and down communication channels, as well as laterally, to achieve the organization's goals. Communication is shared in various forms (verbal, written, and digitally) within teams and company-wide.' (https://www.all thingsic.com)

The increasing interest in IC both as a field of professional practice and as an area of study over the past decade or more is reflected in the steady growth in the number of academic papers and books published on the subject, positioning IC as an interdisciplinary function integrating elements of human resources management, communication, and marketing.

In pragmatic terms, IC can be seen to refer to the discipline of how an organisation speaks and listens to its employees and contractors, and thus it is most effective when it includes two-way methods or channels of communication (see earlier discussion of two-way symmetrical and asymmetrical PR in Chapter 1). The term internal communications (IC) is often used interchangeably with terms such as internal corporate communication; however, organisations and communicators should be wise to the fact that often the most influential voices do not sit in the communications function and may not always be communicating the messages the C-suite would wish to send. IC includes peer-to-peer communication, line management communication, senior management communication, and corporate communication.

Before moving on to explore other important questions about IC, it is helpful to settle on one definition of IC, albeit one synthesised from the various definitions that have been advanced in recent years (see Box 8.2).

Box 8.2 Our definition of internal communication

> 'Internal communication involves the deliberate sharing of information, knowledge, and ideas between members of an organisation, in order to facilitate collaboration, coordination, and mutual comprehension with the goal of ensuring alignment, engagement, and productivity among employees.'

The importance of internal communication

The importance of IC has been increasingly recognised by senior management across the world and has assumed the status of a specialist area of corporate communication/public relations over the past decade. What has driven this rising attention and prominence?

As Verčič et al. (2012) point out, factors such as globalisation, deregulation, and economic crises have led to permanent restructuring, downsizing, outsourcing, mergers and acquisitions, and other kinds of radical changes for employees that have inevitably resulted in a drastic reduction in employee trust in senior management and hence in employee loyalty.

At the same time, organisations have witnessed a growing emphasis on the need to recruit talent and to manage an increasingly changing and ever-evolving workforce. As a consequence, IC has become a critically important function for organisations of all types, particularly those with larger diverse workforces.

IC generally seek to build a sense of belonging and employee identification and commitment towards an organisation through a sustained communication strategy comprising corporate messages and 'storytelling' about the organisation's achievements, history, values, purpose, and how employees can contribute to achieving its goals.

With the attraction and retention of a skilled and committed workforce being such a critical resource for most organisations, merely informing the workforce of what management wants them to know and do is simply not acceptable. If an organisation wants to gain a competitive advantage or increase its share of a market, it needs committed employees willing to go 'the extra mile', and to deliver the organisation's goals. It is here that IC is recognised to have an important part to play.

The key stakeholders in internal communication

The logical focus for IC is on all employees and management levels within an organisation who collectively make up the internal stakeholders audience. Indeed the term 'employee' covers a potentially wide range of positions in terms of both levels of responsibility, and types of roles and formal titles, all of which may vary markedly from organisation to organisation as well as within different industries/sectors.

However, as with external communication, each situation encountered will tend to dictate the particular subset of internal stakeholders that need to be targeted – the target publics. This targeting clearly becomes more complex and sensitive the larger and more diverse the organisation in question. The need for more sophisticated analysis and segmentation of internal target audiences, rather than treating employees/the workforce as a single undifferentiated entity, is more evident when considering larger diverse domestic organisations, or organisations operating on an international basis. Here, perhaps one of the most obvious examples in the UK is the NHS, the largest public sector employer in the UK. Such is the size, geographic footprint, and diversity of services offered within the NHS, not to mention the most obvious distinction between clinicians and the management and administrative staff needed to operate the service that to talk of having a single internal communication strategy for all internal stakeholders and scenarios is almost nonsensical. Something of the scale of the NHS as an employer and site for IC is captured in the employment statistics summarised in Table 8.1.

A further major challenge that IC professionals have encountered in recent years has been the sudden change to remote working caused by Covid-19 and the reluctance of large sections of the workforce to readily return to full-time office-based working practices. Indeed, the whole landscape of office-based work arguably has and is continuing to undergo a major change, with many organisations reorganising the typical 'working week' adopting at least partial remote working policies and appointing 'remote working managers'. Relatively few organisations appear to have returned to full-time office-based work practices, resulting in a significant reduction in the required office footprint across the country. The 'new norm' seems to be some combination of two or three days a week in the office and the balance of the week spent working remotely, connected to a central office by email and web-based apps. This changed pattern of partial remote working obviously has implications for how IC is managed and adds to its importance in maintaining contact with a remotely based workforce. The notion of 'employee engagement' has become all the more important, but also all the more

Table 8.1 Breakdown of Workforce Statistics for NHS in the UK 2023

Category	*October/November 2023*	*October 2022*
All NHS and community health service staff	1,480,880 [+77,653 over 22]	1,403,227
Professionally qualified clinical staff [doctors, nurses, health visitors, etc.]	772,164 [52%] of total headcount and 5% increase over 2022	732,401
Managers and senior managers	39,077 [annual increase of approx. 7%]	36,400
NHS central infrastructure support	111,228 [annual increase of approx. 3.5 %]	107,416
Scientific, therapeutic, and technical staff	166,850 [increase of 4%]	160,329
Percentage of Black and Minority Ethnic [BME] in NHS workforce as a whole	380,108 [26.4% increase approx 2%]	337,038
Percentage of clinicians/medical staff from Black and minority ethnic backgrounds [BME]	Doctors, dentists, and consultants 42% from BME background nurses, midwives, and health visitors 29% from BME background	

Source: NHS Workforce Statistics – www.digital.nhs.uk

challenging to deliver in the new era of greater reliance on remote working practices.

Employee engagement

The notion of 'employee engagement' has been defined as an emotional and intellectual commitment to the organisation (Baumruk 2004; Richman 2006; Shaw 2005). An engaged employee is one who demonstrates energy and effort, is enthusiastic, and is engrossed in their work and desire to impact positively on organisational outcomes.

Obviously, all organisations seek whether deliberately or indirectly to maximise the proportion of engaged employees within the organisation, as this invariably leads to improved productivity, less absenteeism, and hence improved overall performance.

However, it is important to recognise that communication alone cannot create or drive levels of employee engagement. IC can only work to help create or sustain an engaged workforce if the basic workplace environment and terms of employment are conducive to good employee morale and relations – what is sometimes referred to as 'getting the hygiene factors' right' (Herzberg 1959) (see Box 8.3).

Box 8.3 Herzberg's motivation and hygiene factor theory

Frederick Herzberg's theory of motivation, also known as the two-factor theory or motivation-hygiene theory, was developed in the 1960s. According to this theory, there are two groups of factors that have an impact on employee motivation and satisfaction: *motivator factors and hygiene factors*.

Motivator factors are intrinsic factors that lead to *job satisfaction* and motivate employees to perform at higher levels. These factors are related to the work itself and the opportunities for growth and achievement and include challenging work, recognition, responsibility, and opportunities for advancement.

Hygiene factors, on the other hand, are extrinsic factors that, when absent or insufficient, can lead to *job dissatisfaction*. These factors are related to the work environment and include such factors as salary, job security, working conditions, company policies, and relationships with supervisors and colleagues. When hygiene factors are not met, employees can become dissatisfied and their performance may be negatively affected.

Herzberg's theory suggests that getting the right balance between hygiene and motivator factors holds the key to maintaining a productive and satisfied workforce. Here, IC in its 'listening' and 'feedback' roles can help management to remain sensitive to such issues amongst the workforce and perhaps instigate measures to change work patterns, etc., and thereby employee morale and motivation.

Key issues/challenges for internal communication

In many senses, it is almost impossible to identify all the issues/challenges relating to employee–organisation relationships that IC may be called on to help resolve. However, some of the more obvious mainstream challenges and areas of work are outlined here.

Connecting employees within the organisational structure

Internal communicators are normally responsible for ensuring employees at all levels within an organisation understand and then feel connected with their organisation's strategy, purpose, vision, and values. Ideally, a sustained two-way IC strategy will help secure employee 'buy-in' and commitment to realising the organisation's goals.

Today's more enlightened organisations have recognised the need to engage employees at the early stages of any new strategy development, or to at least 'sell-in' the C-suite's vision and strategy to employees to secure their support. Here, face-to-face communication is often the most impactful method and here such tactics might include events, roadshows, experiential activities, and presentations.

Culture: supporting the organisational context/environment

Another area in which IC is often called on to play its part is in communicating a sense of the organisational culture to new and existing staff as well as to external stakeholders. Organisational culture is not easy to pin down and readily describe but is generally recognised as combining elements of the values, norms, beliefs, symbols, and myths that give meaning and identity to an organisation (see Box 8.4). Because of its largely intangible and complex nature, it is not easy to capture and communicate an organisation's distinctive cultural characteristics in a meaningful way. There is also much debate about how far cultures can be designed and imposed on organisations, or whether they develop organically. Whenever senior leaders have sought to influence and change an organisational culture [perhaps after a merger/or major acquisition, or a chosen or enforced radical change of direction], it is generally the case that communication both internal and external is called upon to help communicate, explain, and respond to any opposition to the changes needed. Of course, cultural change cannot be expected to take place overnight and hence will normally require an extended programme of communication linked to other HR policies and 'educational programmes' to build and reinforce understanding of any new values, norms, and expected new 'rules of engagement' both internally and externally.

Box 8.4 Organisational culture

The notion of a recognised organisational culture emerged strongly during the last quarter of 20th century championed by scholars such as Pettigrew (1979) and Schein (1985). Organisational culture refers to the shared values, beliefs, attitudes, norms, and behaviours that characterise an organisation. It is often thought of as the collective understanding and way of thinking that shapes the organisational operating environment and influences how people interact and work together within the organisation. It can include and also reflect such factors as leadership style, communication patterns, work ethics, decision-making processes, and relationships between employees, which, in turn, will shape the overall organisational goals and objectives. It plays a crucial role in determining the overall atmosphere and success of an organisation.

Listening: two-way employee communication

Communication/ PR is generally seen to be most effective when practised as a two-way (symmetrical) function, engaging relevant stakeholders in a 'dialogue' rather than communicating only with them. This is never more so than with IC, where traditionally too little emphasis has tended to be placed on the importance of 'listening' to employees rather than only communicating with them. One of the chief benefits of regular

'listening to the employee voice' is the ability to keep a 'finger on the pulse' of the organisation and take early soundings about potential internal/ workforce-related issues arising. In this sense, internal communicators can help to ensure that the employee voice is heard and can help shape change within the organisation that benefits all.

While these three areas along with supporting employer engagement strategies represent some of the more significant areas of work for the IC function, they represent just a few of many potential areas in which IC can play a valuable role in supporting organisational goals and operational strategies. A listing of other more commonly found areas of work or issues that IC may be called on to support/help tackle are summarised in Box 8.5.

Box 8.5 Examples of issues/problem scenarios typically handled by IC communicator

Changes in working practices/in restructuring the organisation: Helping to explain the rationale for change

Industrial accidents/crises: Handling the internal element of any crisis communication strategy to keep the workforce informed of what is happening and explaining

Industrial disputes: Facilitating liaison between management/HRM and relevant workforce representatives

Employee retention: Ongoing employee communication/relations

Employee recruitment: Helping raise and sustain the organisation's profile in targeted recruitment areas

Local community PR: Local media relations and community involvement programmes

International employee relations: IC strategy to engage employees across the international corporate footprint

Internal communications strategy and implementation

The task of developing an effective IC strategy and tactical plan is in many ways no different, in principle, to that of developing a communication strategy for any other area of organisational communication, which was examined in depth in Chapter 4. In essence, communication planning and delivery comprises the key elements of:

- Problem/situation analysis – analysing the problems/issues faced and defining the communication challenge and role
- Strategy and planning – objective setting, targeting, message and channel determination
- Implementation – taking action and tactical communication delivery
- Evaluation – assessing the impact of the programme.

The key to developing any effective internal or external communication strategy lies in the quality of the initial analysis used to define the nature of the problem situation or scenario to be addressed. This analysis should be conducted from a 'communication perspective', which essentially means determining how the issues/problems identified are likely to impact relevant organisational stakeholders with consequences for the organisation's relations with those groups and its reputation. This analysis then needs to be extended to identify as specifically as possible what role PR/communication might play (if any) in addressing these identified issues. The resulting options might be to adopt a largely passive role with IC simply keeping employees updated on developments. On the other hand, an active interventionist role might be deemed necessary requiring a communication strategy to shape employee perceptions and behaviours with regard to the issue in question.

With this analysis stage safely completed, communicators can press ahead with working up the detailed strategy and implementation plan starting with clear objectives and specific targeting and rolling out into a carefully constructed message and media/channel programme, and of course, making provision to evaluate the outcomes. You can refresh your understanding of the communication planning process by revisiting Chapter 4.

Typical PR/communication tactics used in internal communication

Employee communication can involve both formal and informal tactics.

Formal methods/activities can include newsletters, workplace posters, noticeboards, face-to-face meetings at various levels, annual reports, and memoranda and other in-house notifications. Moreover, in today's increasingly digitalised world, many of these traditional tools have been replaced or augmented by digital variants. So, for example, most of the larger organisations have established intranet and dedicated email servers to disseminate up-to-date information to employees throughout the organisation rather than relying on noticeboards and periodically distribute.

Informal channels in the form of ongoing interaction and conversations within employee peer groups and between managers and employees often occur on a day-to-day basis in most organisations. Here, the openness of the prevailing organisation's culture and even the physical layout and structure of an organisation's buildings (hygiene factors) can play an important part in encouraging a facilitating informal and formal communication both horizontally between peer groups and vertically between employees and the various tiers of management. It is often the communication through these informal channels that is seen to have greater credibility than information distributed via formal organisational channels. Moreover, what is widely recognised as '*the grapevine*' exists in virtually all organisations comprised of rumours, gossip, and half-truths, which because the information is often unfiltered and passed through many hands can be quite distorted. However, it is the unofficial, unfiltered nature of this type of communication that gives its influence no matter how accurate or not. From an IC management perspective, it is important to try to tap into this grapevine communication to be aware of what is being said and take action to rebut or challenge misunderstandings and untruths about the organisation.

Internal communication evaluation

The final stage in the IC process is that of evaluation, which like all organisational activity is vitally important in order to assess whether planned outcomes have been achieved, what has worked or not worked, and where improvement in communication might be needed. Here, the use of employee surveys and focus groups can be used to collect feedback from the key target groups. One key tool for internal communicators is the ability to carry out an internal communication audit (see Box 8.6). This assessment of the current situation with regard to IC is intended to identify what is and is not working, and hence how things can be improved. Here, tools such as the ICQ10 survey developed by Kevin Ruck (2022) of the PR Academy can help to identify where communications and OD professionals can work together to improve the employee offer and communication experience.

Box 8.6 Communication audits

A communication audit [CA] is a systematic process of evaluating and assessing the effectiveness of an organisation's communication strategies, channels, and messages and to identify areas of improvement.

A CA will normally examine all aspects of an organisation's internal and external communication activities, and channels including email, social media, newsletters, press releases and all employee communication activity. An audit assesses how these channels are used by communicators and target audiences, how well they align with the organisation's goals and objectives, and how effectively they reach and engage the target audience. CAs also focus on examining the clarity, consistency, and quality of the organisation's messages and ensure they are in line with the organisation's values, brand identity, and desired image. Typically, a CA will gather the required data from surveys, face-to-face forums and meetings, social media posts, and intranet comments.

References and additional reading

Baumruk, R. (2004). The missing link: The role of employee engagement in business success. *Workspan, 47*, 48–52.

Herzberg, F. (1959). *The motivation to work.* New York: Wiley and Sons. https://www.cipd.org/uk/knowledge/factsheets/engagement-factsheet/

Pettigrew, A.M. (1979). On studying organisational cultures. *Administrative Science Quarterly, 24*(4), 570–581.

Richman, A. (2006). Everyone wants an engaged workforce how can you create it? *Workspan, 49*, 36–39.

Ruck, K. (January 5, 2022). *ICQ10: Ten questions for internal communications surveys*. [Accessed on 22 February 2024] https://pracademy.co.uk/insights/icq10-ten-questions-for-internal-communication-and-organisational-engagement/

Shein, E. (1985). *Organisational culture and leadership.* San Francisco: Jossey Bass.

Shaw, K. (2005). An engagement strategy process for communicators. *Strategic Communication Management, 9*(3), 26–29.

Verčič, A.T., Verčič, D. and Sriramesh, K. (2012). Internal communication: Definition parameters, and the future. *Public Relations Review, 38*(2) June, 223–230.

9 Crisis management

Barbara DeSanto

Box 9.1 Essentials summary

No organisation can necessarily avoid a crisis affecting them at some time. What they can do is put in place crisis plans that can be activated when required. While crises are generally sudden, unexpected events with potentially significant organisational repercussions, pre-crisis planning is essential to survive such events. This chapter addresses three stages of crisis management: (1) pre-planning, (2) specific actions to take when a crisis breaks, and (3) post-crisis mitigation and learning.

Crises can take many different forms, ranging from natural disasters (e.g. hurricanes, earthquakes, and floods) to industrial accidents, corporate mismanagement and malpractices, and increasingly, acts of terrorism. The chapter examines how organisations can best prepare to handle whatever form of crisis they might encounter and what specific processes they can put in place to minimise the impact of crises if and when they hit. Controlling the information flow during and after a crisis emerges as the most important principle in effective crisis management. The difficulty of reconciling the best practice guidance for crisis handling from a PR/communication perspective with that of an organisation's legal advisors emerges clearly. In an often litigation-dominated culture, it is usually mistakenly the legal team whose arguments prevail only for the organisation to discover that they then pay a very high price in longer-term reputation damage.

Introduction

Crises come in different forms, ranging from natural disasters such as hurricanes, floods, and earthquakes, which can have devastating consequences for the areas and populations affected, to industrial accidents such as the huge

DOI: 10.4324/9781003129004-12

environmental disaster resulting from the Deepwater Horizon oil spill in the Gulf of Mexico after the explosion on a BP oil rig in 2010 or more recently, the collapse of the Baltimore bridge after a container ship that had gone out of control collided with the bridge. Crises can also arise from financial mismanagement of a company, which may lead, in the worst-case scenario, to its collapse, such as what happened to Lehman Brothers, sparking the notorious sub-prime mortgage crisis in 2008. Corporate mismanagement or fraudulent behaviour can equally cause a major crisis of confidence in an organisation. Although not an entirely new phenomenon, countries around the world have all witnessed an escalation in the scale of terrorist crisis incidents in recent years, causing death and destruction on an unprecedented scale, perhaps most notably the infamous 9/11 attack on the Twin Towers in New York. Not only does such terrorism cause the loss of life and physical damage but it also creates a heightened sense of fear and uncertainty among the population, which is precisely what the terrorists are seeking to do! One common thread that runs through all these different types of crises is a desperate search for information about events as they unfold among those directly affected and those reporting on or viewing from a distance. It is how this information is assembled, controlled, and disseminated as appropriate that lies at the centre of effective crisis management. Box 9.2 outlines one notorious example of 'domestic terrorism' and the crisis it sparked.

Box 9.2 Oklahoma City Bombing 1995

19 April 1995 started as a beautiful spring day in Oklahoma City in the centre of the United States. In a matter of minutes, a bomb exploded in the Alfred P. Murrah Federal Building, killing 168 people and maiming hundreds of others.

A decorated American soldier, Timothy McVeigh, masterminded and built the bomb in a Ryder truck, drove it to Oklahoma City, and ignited the fuse at 9:02. His motivation: Avenging what he saw as the U.S. federal government's invasion of the Branch Davidian cult compound in Waco, Texas two years earlier.

The Murrah Building was the regional headquarters for several U.S. federal agencies, including the Federal Bureau of Investigation (FBI), the Social Security Administration (SSA), and the Housing and Urban Development Agency (HUD). Especially, heartbreaking were the 19 children killed and dozens of others injured in the building's daycare centre.

To date, it was the most devastating domestic terrorist act in the U.S. In addition to the loss of life and injury in the Murrah Building, buildings in a several-mile radius suffered damage from the blast.

And, because the state of Oklahoma has a relatively small population of 3 million residents, nearly everyone in the state knew someone who was affected by the bombing. One of the learning outcomes from this bombing was that the action of the Oklahoma City police, fire, and first-response agencies came from the state's extensive experience with deadly tornadoes.

This crisis was also the impetus and example for preparing more domestic terrorism events.

Recognising when an organisation is in a crisis is a matter of assessing the impact of an event. Here, operating in their 'boundary spanning role', PR practitioners may get an early warning of potential crises looming through their monitoring of ongoing relevant issues, which most of the larger organisations will have in place as a critical responsibility for the PR team/practitioners. However, some issues may suddenly turn into crises due to unexpected events. For example, 'safety' will always be an ongoing issue for shipping and freight transportation companies, but few might have anticipated the sudden upsurge of attacks on shipping attempting to pass through the Suez Canal by Yemeni Houthi groups following the outbreak of fighting in the Gaza strip after Hamas terrorists attacked Israeli settlements. As an immediate response, many shipping companies have opted to avoid the Suez Canal and send their vessels on long trips around Africa, significantly adding to supply chain delays and costs. While perhaps an extreme example, other issues that may seem relatively stable and even benign can develop into a crisis if not dealt with in a timely manner. Also, not all issues will have the same impact on every concerned organisation. It may depend very much on the organisation's position, resources, ability to withstand any fallout from an issue, etc. Determining when to take action about an issue is a judgement call to prevent it from becoming a full-blown crisis. Equally, an organisation doesn't want to escalate an issue into a crisis, which, if left unattended, could have been avoided.

Categories of crises

A crisis is an event with significant consequences/outcomes that can substantially affect an organisation's financial, political, or social character, or ultimately, its survival. Table 9.1 categorises the traditional types of crises that might occur.

Crisis management

Given that any organisation can, for a variety of reasons, find itself facing some form of crisis – whether physical, economic, or political, which, in the

Table 9.1 Newsom Crisis Typology

Crisis source	Violent cataclysmic Immediate loss of life or property	Non-violent: Sudden upheaval, but damages, if any, are delayed
Act of nature	Forest fires, earthquakes, mudslides, hurricanes, tornadoes, floods	Droughts, epidemics, diseases such as H1N1, Covid-19, flu, Ebola
Intentional	Acts of terrorism that result in loss of life and/or destruction of property such as the US 9/11 attack	Bomb and product tampering threats, hostile takeovers, insider trading resulting in large and/or investment losses such as Enron
Unintentional	Explosions, fires, leaks, and other accidents, such as the BP Texas Gulf deepwater drilling oil spill	Process or product problems with delayed consequences, such as VW emissions scandal or the 2010 US egg recall

Source: Adapted from Doug Newsom, 'A Crisis Typology', paper presented at the Latin American & Caribbean Communication Conference, Florida, 8 February 1988

worst case, could threaten the organisation's very survival, it makes sense to develop and maintain a well-thought crisis plan that can be put into action should circumstances dictate it is needed. A crisis management plan is a structured approach that outlines how an organisation will respond to a crisis or emergency situation. It involves identifying potential risks, developing strategies to address them, and implementing protocols to manage the crisis effectively. Effective crisis management arguably extends beyond simply handling the challenges and demands of an immediate crisis when it hits but includes the pre-crisis stage of issues monitoring and crisis preparedness as well as the post-crisis follow-up of conducting a 'post-mortem' on how well the crisis management team handled events and what the impact of the crisis has been on the organisation and its reputation. These three critical stages of crisis management are captured in Figure 9.1.

In principle, a crisis management plan will follow a similar pattern to any other area of communication, which we argued could be captured in the CMACIE framework we examined earlier in Chapter 4. In short, comprising an issue/crisis *analysis phase* followed by the *choice* of appropriate crisis communication strategy and tactics, the *implementation* of that strategy, and finally, the *evaluation* of the outcomes of the crisis communication plan in terms of how successfully it enabled the organisation to navigate its way through the crisis and what the impact has been for the organisation and its future. Like all functional areas of communication, 'best practice' means using standardised models and adapting them to the specific circumstances faced and responding to the needs of the particular stakeholder groups involved in the crisis situation. While we have stressed the importance of the initial

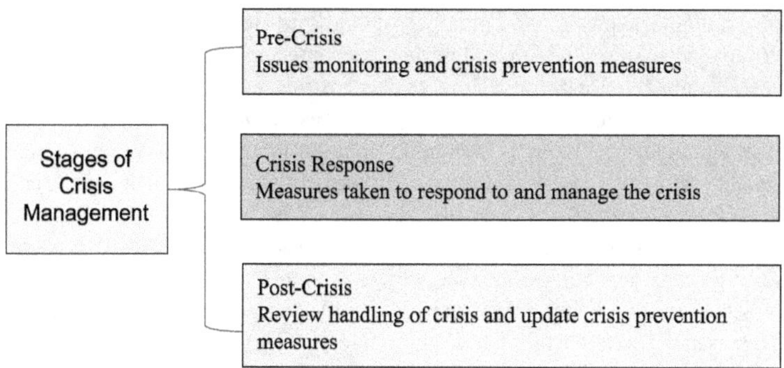

Figure 9.1 Stages in Crisis Management.

stage of communication analysis, which is often critical in establishing what the priorities in the communication strategy should be and which stakeholder relationships are particularly crucial to the success of the strategy, arguably, this initial analysis (crisis preparedness) stage is absolutely critical in crisis management planning.

Crisis preparation best practices

The first step in any crisis planning process is to identify and quantify the potential impact of everything that could damage the organisation. Here, this analysis will vary from industry to industry and will also depend on the organisation's involvement in that industry. So, for example, an organisation that supplies upholstery and cushioning for seating in Airbus or Boeing aircraft will have a very risk issues profile and issue analysis to say Rolls Royce or Generic Electric (GE) responsible for supplying the engines for these aircraft. Similarly, organisations supplying major accounting software systems and solutions to businesses might not envisage facing any physical issues due to their 'products' performance, but systems failure can have profound impacts on their clients' businesses and, in turn, on their clients' relationships with their stakeholders. The recent furore over the now acknowledged failings of Fujitsu Horizon software that was installed in most UK post offices and which appeared to reveal widespread fraud by sub-postmasters over many years has now cast a serious 'cloud' over Fujitsu's handling of events and their failure to 'come clean' about the shortcomings of their software.

Crises such as the Fujitsu post office scandal fall into the category of crises resulting from major systems failure, compounded by corporate malpractice and potentially even fraudulent behaviour. The financial services sector is one that has experienced a number of crises over the years as a result of the exposure of a number of high-profile financial scandals involving vast sums of money that has been misappropriated and, in some cases, embezzled with devasting effects for the individuals and organisations involved. Here, such high-profile cases as Enron, E.F. Hutton, Lehman Brothers, and most recently, the Sam Bankman-Fried FEX crypto exchange scandal illustrate the potentially devastating impact that such crises can have for all involved.

So, each industry will have its own potential risk issue profile, and PR teams need to construct a relevant issues-risk–stakeholder matrix (see Chapter 6), which needs to be continually updated to reflect any relevant changes in the organisation's external or internal environments. This may range from physical disasters/events to internal accidents, systems failures, and human/employee malpractice, which could potentially damage and derail the organisation's operations and impact its reputation and even long-term survival.

Of course, even the most far-sighted issues analysts cannot hope to anticipate every potential crisis, particularly those that strike out of the blue, such as physical/environmental disasters such as the Baltimore bridge collapse or the wildfires that have swept through parts of Australia and earlier Southern Europe due to the prolonged extreme high temperatures attributed to climate change. Here, constant issues monitoring and subsequent evaluation should lead to a reappraisal of risk issues over time, allowing more effective crisis preparedness measures to be implemented.

Stakeholder/issue analysis

Once a set of relevant issues/sources of crises has been identified, the next step is to prioritise them from the most to the least likely. If this process has been conducted using an issues-stakeholder matrix (see Table 6.1) or a similar tool, then the analysis will also have linked the issues to the related stakeholders who must be prioritised according to their importance and involvement. Here, as with other areas of PR analysis, a listing of key stakeholders should be readily available. For example, where physical accidents figure prominently in the organisation's risk profile, the crisis management team should ensure that they have access to a comprehensive listing of all employees based on each of the organisation's sites/plants so that in the event of an industrial accident those injured and safe can readily be compiled and communicated to relevant family members before the media get hold of such information. Again, the broad range of potential stakeholders for crisis analysis will include:

- Media, including traditional and social media, will always be an important stakeholder group. Word spreads instantaneously. Who is the source of this information is critical, as it sets the tone for the coverage and the narrative of who is in charge.

- Employees are often overlooked during crisis times. Yet each employee has family and/or friends that immediately contact that employee to find out what happened. As much transparency as possible is necessary for this group.
- Lawyers are necessary in this situation, as they will be the ones who consider potential liabilities. Lawyers and communicators often need help with the court of public opinion, which develops quickly in a crisis, versus the court of law, which can take months or years to conclude blame and damages that often severely impact organisations.
- Emergency personnel, including fire, police, and health service.
- The local community around an organisation's plant or facilities, many of whom may have family who work for the organisation or may run businesses that depend on the organisation to a large degree for trade.
- Relevant special interest or pressure groups with an active interest in the organisation's work and output or policies – particularly those associated with extraction or chemical industries, which are likely to be under constant scrutiny by environmental pressure groups.

Of course, once an actual crisis begins to emerge or, in the case of an accident or event, fit the organisation, the broad list of stakeholders needs to be crystallised into a particular targeted listing, which itself may become something of a changing set as events unfold.

Identifying these key groups is the first step in creating a core crisis management team. While one list of team members is created, others, such as specific experts depending on the nature of the crisis, may be added as the crisis develops.

The crisis communication team and action plans

Once it becomes clear that the organisation is facing a crisis of whatever type, the next step is to call together the crisis management team, which, depending on the type and scale of the crisis, may include specialist experts from other functions such as engineering or life science, etc. who can field any technical questions that the media or other inquisitors might raise. In organising the crisis management team and establishing its modus operandi, a number of critical questions/decisions need to be addressed:

- Who should convene the crisis management team, and under what conditions?
- Where crisis team members should meet, both in-person and online?
- Identification of the lead communication spokesperson
- What the initial statement should say, including safety measures?
- Plans for further information release

Once the framework is determined, the crisis communication team can develop the following tools for distributing information if/when a crisis develops:

- Dark websites with pre-created details depending on the crisis
- Sample news releases, social media posts, talking points
- Organisation's history and location(s)
- Any particular type of organisational mechanics, operations, and technical information
- Regulations and laws that may apply (especially safety standards)
- Guidelines for who talks to whom, when, and about what in what format (online, in-person, on-site, etc.)
- Executive and managerial biographies
- Previous media coverage, including warnings and bad regulation reviews.
- List of names, phone numbers, and social media contacts of all relevant spokespeople, from executives on down
- Governmental, political, and legal jurisdictions because of different rules and liabilities.

Once the plans and scenarios are developed, they should be written down and stored in multiple formats (remember, power outages wreak havoc on digital systems), shared, practised, and updated on a regular basis. Being able to access such information rapidly and efficiently if the crisis is happening is vitally important since it helps demonstrate that the organisation is 'in control' of the situation.

Crisis action phase

Moving on from crisis preparation to the action/implementation stage, the following guideline points need to be borne in mind, particularly during the early hours of any crisis:

- The action phase of a crisis happens fast and is often chaotic no matter how much you plan, and there will be lots of information holes, conflicting information, and speculation.
- It is critical that the organisation takes control of the narrative and the situation first. That means addressing the situation even without any specific information. The spokesperson must be as forthcoming as possible and able to produce any relevant players, such as CEOs and managers, as quickly as possible.
- At the stage where the crisis erupts, no one may know what has happened. It is okay for the organisation to say it doesn't know everything that happened and does not have any specific details.
- It is vital to be truthful and establish immediately how and when you will share information as it becomes available. Then follow through.

- It is essential to share with employees any information you share with the media immediately.
- Particularly where there might be severe injuries or fatalities involved, management must show that the organisation has a 'human' face, including concerns for the safety of the organisation's employees and the wider public who might be affected.

Crisis communication scholar Timothy Coombs offers some key guidelines for crisis communication channel best practices (see Box 9.3).

Box 9.3 Coombs' crisis communication channel preparation best practices

- Be prepared to use part of your current website to address crisis concerns.
- Be prepared to use the intranet or enterprise social networking to reach employees and other key stakeholders during a crisis.
- Be prepared to use a mass notification system to reach employees and key stakeholders during a crisis.
- Be prepared to utilise your existing social media channels to respond to your crisis.

Citation: *Https//instituteforpr.org/crisis-management-and-communications/*

Ongoing crisis action phase tactics/actions

As the crisis progresses, ensuring the crisis communication team members have backup is important. This is a time of high trauma for all involved, often chaotic communication, and one person cannot handle it all for any length of time. Communicators must also put the most relevant spokespeople in front of the media. The CEO is not always the best person to be on camera, nor is the uninformed employee who was part of the crisis scene.

Keeping good written notes on who said what to whom, when, and how is essential as the crisis progresses. This helps avoid conflicting information being disseminated and could provide important information for later examination when the crisis response is examined.

Outside players, such as fire, police, and regulators must be consulted and 'kept in the loop' with copies of all crisis coverage. The media will invariably seek the emergency services for comment and further information. Sometimes, where a crisis occurs can significantly influence who and how the crisis management process is handled. See Box 9.4 for an example of this consideration.

Box 9.4 Where the crisis happens

Public Information Officer Barbara DeSanto was part of a complex government/private crisis plan for the Southwest Regional Airport in Fort Myers, Florida. The county in which the city is located is a combination of government property, private property, regional, and city and county land. Each of these legal entities has primary jurisdiction in their dedicated lands. What this meant for crisis planning for any airline disaster, including crashes, was who was in charge of the crisis communication management depending entirely on where the crash happened. The crisis plan for the Fort Myers airport included a plan of action and chain of command for each designated, legally recognised location. This meant there were seven plans; each detailed the chain of command and the steps to be taken. Once a year, all of the different entities got together to practice the plans.

Once a crisis becomes visible, the crisis team must swing into action, reacting to events usually with incomplete information and seeking to be proactive. The team can respond by dealing with what is happening in real time while adapting previously developed crisis plans/scenarios to manage the coming days. This visible stage is generally the shortest stage because, in large part, the media will move on after the initial event, and the information gets repetitive. The often relatively short timescale for this stage doesn't diminish the importance of managing every minute of this visibility; the effects will almost certainly linger on through litigation and media updates. In many cases, the crisis label itself (i.e. 9/11, Hurricane Katrina) brings up the event all over again.

It's normally impossible to predict how long the active crisis stage will last; the goal is to manage the situation as quickly and effectively as possible. This includes communicating with all affected stakeholders and the media.

Here, an important point to remember is that every statement and action can impact the organisation's credibility and reputation, sometimes long after the crisis action subsides.

This is often where the legal and crisis communication teams have differing viewpoints, as communicators want to share as much information as possible, while attorneys are concerned with legal ramifications. Before a crisis occurs, communicators need to liaise with the organisation's legal team and remind them that as much transparency as possible has the power to mitigate the legal consequences post-crisis.

Another frequent disagreement between communicators and attorneys is whether the organisation should express concern or sympathy for the crisis victims and, if so, how much. Here, attorneys will often resist because of the potential of such expressions being used in potential lawsuits as evidence of guilt on the part of the organisation. Research suggests that carefully crafted statements showing the organisation's compassion and recognition of the situation help the organisation in legal cases. Here, Coombs summarises guidance for how organisations should respond to media and other enquiries during the early phase of a crisis (see Box 9.5).

Box 9.5 Coombs' initial crisis response practice points

- Be quick and try to have an initial response within the first hour.
- Be accurate by carefully checking all the facts.
- Be consistent by keeping spokespeople informed of crisis events and key message points.
- Make public safety the number one priority.
- Use all available communication channels, including social media, websites, the intranet, and mass notification systems.
- Provide some expression of concern/sympathy for the victims.
- Remember to include employees in the initial response.
- Be ready to provide stress and trauma counselling to crisis victims and their families, including employees.

Citation: *Https//instituteforpr.org/crisis-management-and-communications/*. Accessed 11 December 2023

Post-crisis best practice

Once the worst effects of a crisis have passed, organisations tend to want to 'get back to normal' as quickly as possible, reducing the negative after-effects on the stock price and investment losses and seeking to rebuild goodwill with stakeholders quickly.

This is not always so easy to achieve because there may be stakeholders who want to keep the issue alive until they have reached what they consider a fair resolution, where there has been noticeable damage or injury to some parties affected by the crisis, there may be a protracted period involving legal action, court cases, negotiations, and external investigations leading to fault-finding and assigning responsibility which are all part of this post-crisis stage.

As the event's visible, 'front-page effects' subside, the PR/communication team needs to immediately debrief, assessing what parts of the crisis plan went well and what parts went awry and failed to work as effectively as expected. This post-crisis deconstruction and debriefing, including documenting the process and the outcomes to date, is essential to making changes in future plans. Failure to conduct this debrief promptly risks losing valuable information and increases the possibility of future blunders.

While the coverage might have subsided, it's important to keep stakeholders apprised of ongoing corrective action and crisis investigation. This is part of controlling the narrative, reinforcing the idea that the organisation is the best source of credible information.

Equally important is the growing phenomenon of paying tribute to the victims of the crisis, often by creating memorials and conducting anniversary events. This is the place for an organisation to show its human side and reinforce any corrective actions it has taken from the crisis. Again Coombs (2007, 2014; Coombs and Holladay 2022) offers a useful summary of the key post-crisis best practices.

Box 9.6 Coombs' post-crisis-phase best practices

- Keep stakeholders updated on the progression of recovery efforts, including any corrective measures being taken and any investigations being conducted.
- Analyse the crisis management effort for lessons and integrate those into the organisation's crisis management system.
- Scan the Internet channels for online memorials.
- Consult with victims and their families to determine the organisation's role in any anniversary events or memorials.

Citation: *Https//instituteforpr.org/crisis-management-and-communications/*. Accessed 11 December 2023

References and additional reading

Coombs, T. (2007). Protecting organization reputations during a crisis: The development and application of situational crisis communication theory. *Corporate Reputation Review*, 10(3), 163–176.

Coombs, T. (2023). Crisis management and communications: Updated September 2014. Institute for Public Relations [Accessed 11 December] http://instituteforpr.org

Coombs, W.T. and Holladay, S. (2022). *The handbook of crisis communication*. Chichester, W. Sussex: John Wiley & Sons Ltd.

Additional reading

Griffin, A. (2014). *Crisis, issues and reputation management: A handbook for PR and communication professionals.* London: Kogan Page.

Lukaszewski, J. (2013). Lukaszewski on crisis communication: What your CEO needs to know about reputation, risk, and crisis management. Rothstein Associates, Incorporated, March 2013.

10 Public relations and public affairs

Peter Osborne

Box 10.1 Essentials summary

Public affairs (PA) is generally a function predominantly found in larger organisations where it offers unique strategic, analytical, problem-solving, and environmental-scanning expertise to senior management to cope with the challenges of an increasingly complex and internationalised world. In essence, PA sits at the interface between business, citizens, and government, serving as an outward-facing 'intelligence function' – constantly scanning the broader political, economic, and societal environments to identify issues arising that might play out negatively or offer opportunities for the organisation going forward. PA focuses, in particular, on issues more likely to give rise to potential legislative and regulatory changes that might impact organisational policies and operations. PA then works to try to influence relevant legislators and regulators, often through well-orchestrated lobbying campaigns designed to try to shape the framing of their policies so as to minimise the impact on the organisation. Here, it is important to acknowledge that public affairs cannot thrive in some environments, notably those with no free press/media, or in autocratic regimes where the government process offers little opportunity for corporate or citizen representation in the framing of legislation. It is notable that because of the far-reaching potential impact of the types of issues PA typically focuses on, PA generally has a far more elevated status amongst senior management than public relations, despite the fact that conceptually at least PA is a subset of the PR function.

DOI: 10.4324/9781003129004-13

Defining public affairs

Academics and public affairs practitioners alike struggle to agree on what the practice and discipline of public affairs (PA) is. There is considerable ambiguity, even an element of mystery, surrounding what is arguably often seen as a specialist sub-function of public relations focused around influencing political decisions, and the actions of Government. For many commentators outside the world of PR, public affairs is often seen as a rather clandestine activity, usually concerned with promoting the special interests of one organisation or faction over the general good through legislative or governmental actions.

From this perspective, public affairs professionals are often seen to operate predominantly as political lobbyists, and in this guise are often portrayed in the media as practising the 'dark arts'. But a more balanced argument acknowledges that PA advocacy or lobbying is essential for healthy democracies (see Box 10.2) by ensuring that stakeholders and the public receive appropriate information so that they can make informed political decisions.

Box 10.2 Lobbying

Political lobbying is a fundamental part of the democratic process, enabling individuals or groups to attempt to influence government decisions. Lobbying involves communicating/presenting persuasive arguments in various forms to policymakers to try to convince them to support/adopt specific policies that align with the interests of the lobbyists. Transparency and accountability are key principles in ethical lobbying practices. Lobbyists should disclose their clients, objectives, and activities to the public and comply with relevant laws and regulations governing lobbying activities – the most high profile of which was the 'Principles of Public Life', produced by the Nolan Committee in 1995. These were intended as guidelines for ethical standards expected of all public office holders.

Three possible definitions of PA are summarised as follows:

[1] Most definitions tend to agree that public affairs involve managing an organisation's 'relationship with its stakeholders'. For example, the Public Affairs Council proposes that *PA is 'the management function responsible for monitoring and managing a corporation's external business*

environment' and '*integrates government affairs; advocacy; communications; environmental, social and corporate governance; and issues management to influence public policy, build a strong brand and find common ground with stakeholders'*.

[2] The Public Affairs Network agrees that '*PA describes an organisation's relationship with stakeholders'* – '*individuals or groups with an interest in the organisation's affairs, such as politicians, civil servants, customers, and local communities, clients, shareholders, trade associations, think tanks, business groups, charities, unions and the media'*.

[3] The UK Local Government Association Network emphasises the political that public affairs is *'an organisation's approach to building and maintaining relationships with key stakeholders, particularly those in the political or governmental sphere'*.

There are clearly differences and similarities between all three of these definitions – so where do we go from here?

Acknowledging the lack of consensus about a definition of public affairs, Moss et al. (2012) suggest that public affairs '*may refer to how organisations manage the "nexus" between business, politics, and communication*'; that is,

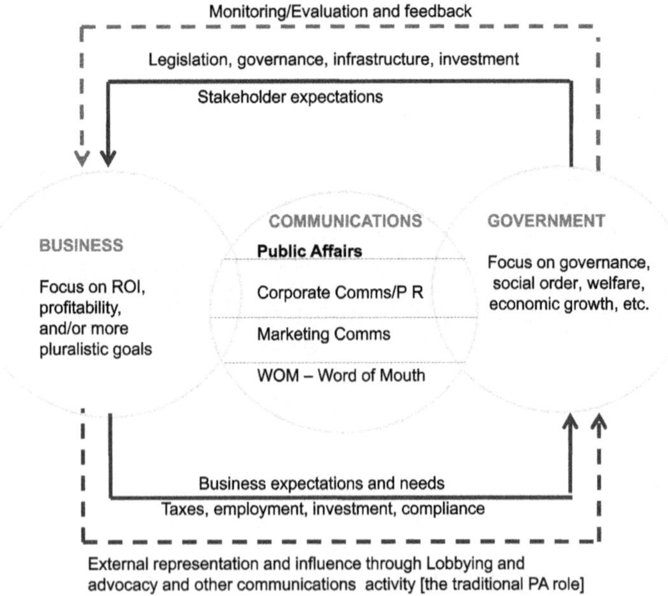

Figure 10.1 The Nexus of Business, Government Interests and the Mediating Role of Public Affairs /Communication.

it suggests a broader involvement with the management of issues that affect the range of corporate stakeholders (see Figure 10.1).

The terminology used in different contexts can also be a source of further confusion about public affairs. So, for example, some organisations and media use terms such as corporate affairs or regulatory affairs. In the latter case, the notion of *regulatory affairs* is normally treated as a specialist application of public affairs concerned primarily with the compliance of all involved with standards and rules, for example, in the healthcare sector or financial services where compliance with standards and rules by all professionals involved in each respective field is critically important. Professional bodies such as TOPRA (The Organisation for Professionals in Regulatory Affairs) have assumed increasing importance over the years in helping organisations to set standards and ensure that all professionals understand the importance of adhering to them.

Is public affairs understood by colleagues?

Anecdotal and academic evidence suggests that public affairs is often confused with PR or corporate communications and tends not to be viewed as a distinct function in its own right. And yet arguably, public affairs can sometimes be viewed as 'game-changing' in a world driven by globalisation issues – elevating the function to a high status. The increasing politicisation of all aspects of both the business world and society as a whole in recent years has seen organisations of all complexions turning to public affairs to try to exercise influence on impending legislation, regulation, and politics that is likely to affect their future prospects in some significant way. On the surface at least, it appears that the advancement in public affairs thinking and expertise has occurred most notably in Western countries, and in particular in Europe and the US where there has been explosive growth in the number of public affairs consultants at work. However, the increasing internationalisation of business and the impact of social media worldwide have forced many internationally based businesses and not-for-profit organisations to extend their PA efforts to encompass a broad international landscape.

While public affairs is a practice that for many remains shrouded in mystery and misunderstanding, there seems little doubt that public affairs has assumed increasing importance in the communications mix of larger organisations in an increasingly complex and interconnected world. The UK CIPR's 'State of PR 2020/21' report stated that demand for public affairs increased by 18% as organisations sought increasingly to engage with key stakeholders during the recent Covid pandemic. Indeed, this author's own experience over 30 years working at a senior level in corporate communications is of growing prominence and influence of the public affairs function in larger, often international, highly regulated organisations operating in the nuclear, utilities, environment, and health and social care sectors. In such sectors, organisations tend to operate in complex, turbulent, and often highly regulated environments where senior management has recognised the need for public affairs expertise and skills to help navigate through what is often perceived to be a very hostile regulatory environment.

Public affairs practitioner roles and specialist agencies

According to *Public Affairs Networking*, public affairs practitioners 'may specialise in media relations, campaign management, local government or "Parliamentary Bills", whilst others will work across the spectrum of communications'. (https://www.publicaffairsnetworking.com/about-public-affairs-networking.php)

Generally, public affairs practitioners tend to work in one or other of five settings:

- 'in-house' for a company, trade association, or charity;
- as an advisor for a political consultancy working with several clients;
- for a trade union, or political, or issue-based organisation;
- for a government agency or in local government;
- or as a freelancer;

So clearly a wide variety of opportunities exist for public affairs professionals across the private, public, and not-for-profit sectors. Public affairs practitioners will aim to take a strategic view of the organisation they work for, focus on key stakeholders and corporate goals, be policy-oriented, coordinate sector research, do analysis, and often engage in lobbying on behalf of their organisation. Effective PA professionals need to be able to quickly analyse and summarise complex information or data for various audiences, as is the ability to see the 'bigger picture'. In some cases, organisations may choose or prefer to hire a PA agency to handle specific projects rather than retain a full-time PA professional(s) or may hire an agency to provide tactical support to an in-house PA staff member. Of course, in-house PA professionals are more likely to have intimate knowledge of an organisation and its background and, hence, may be up to speed a lot more quickly in handling issues as they arise. On the other hand, external consultants may bring a wider range of background experiences from other industries into play, which might aid them in devising creative solutions to the challenges faced. In short, each organisation (and situation) may have different preferences when it comes to decisions about whether to use in-house and external PA expertise.

So summarising what we know about public affairs

- PA is a broad term that encompasses the relationship between organisations (inc businesses, and not-for-profit organisations, citizens, and government entities.

- PA involves managing communication, building relationships, and influencing public policy and decision-making processes.
- PA requires a deep understanding of public policy, communication strategies, and stakeholder engagement.
- PA plays a key role in shaping public opinion, influencing legislation through lobbying, and building positive relationships between organisations and the communities they serve.
- PA helps organisations navigate complex regulatory environments, manage crises effectively, and advocate for their interests.
- Organisations may hire their own full-time PA professionals or hire specialist agencies/freelancers to handle projects as they arise, or a combination of the two.

The key stakeholders for public affairs

PA focuses on a range of key stakeholders that are derived from and reflect the key challenges and scope of the role it plays on behalf of organisations. These include (for UK-based organisations):

- National government officials including elected government and opposition Ministers and MPs, special advisors, and civil servants
- Local government counsellors and officials
- Depending on the scope of the organisation's operations and where relevant, the equivalent overseas international government bodies and regulatory authorities
- Relevant pressure and special interest and community groups
- Other industry sector members with a shared interest in any regulatory or legal issue being considered
- Key industry bodies (CBI, IOD, etc.)
- Relevant legal and regulatory bodies
- Key media and social media journalists and social media influencers
- And the general public/public opinion

A similar analysis would be conducted where organisations based in other countries identify and prioritise the equivalent government and other stakeholder groups.

Key issues/challenges for public affairs

The issues and challenges that the PA professional is asked to help resolve are normally ones that have significant potential consequences for an organisation, whether in terms of its operation in strategically important areas, reputation either regionally, nationally, or, in some cases, on the international stage, or, in highly regulated industries, its 'licence to operate'. Issues normally arise as a consequence of one of three main types of scenarios:

(1) As a consequence of organisational policies and actions that have actual or perceived adverse impacts on particular stakeholders – for example, plant closures, effluent discharge into waterways, proposed new mine or fracking developments
(2) As a consequence of the actions of particular stakeholder groups that threaten to disrupt or otherwise adversely impact the operation of organisations – for example, local protest groups' actions over airport expansion plans at Heathrow and Manchester airports; recent 'Just Stop Oil' protest movement
(3) As a consequence of government policies or other external events that threaten to adversely impact an organisation's future strategies, operations, and/or reputation – for example, government increased windfall taxation on oil and gas companies' profits, regulatory opposition to mergers/acquisitions such as the Microsoft takeover bid for Activism Blizzard, and perhaps most notably the impact of the imposition of national and international lockdown measures as a result of the Covid-19 pandemic.

In all instances, the key task for PA focuses on monitoring public opinion, analysing government and regulatory policy trends, and engaging with government officials, community leaders, and other key stakeholders to help identify and ideally anticipate the trajectory of key issues that the organisation needs to address in some way. From this analysis, PA professionals will then seek to determine how the organisation might best respond to mitigate any adverse impact of specific issues.

Of course, not all issues may have serious consequences for every organisation potentially affected, nor will the consequences of an issue play out the same way for each organisation. It may all depend on how well prepared an organisation is, what resources it has available, and in the case of potential reputational damage, how much 'reputational credit it has in the bank' with its stakeholders. All organisations make mistakes and may misjudge how certain issues may unfold. The key to managing and surviving through such scenarios without too much damage is generally by sustaining open two-way lines of communication with all relevant stakeholders, communicating what, why, and how the organisation is dealing with the issue at hand while acknowledging its responsibility to its key stakeholder groups. This stage of issues analysis is critical to determining the options for an organisation going forward and determining the most appropriate PA/ communication strategy to adopt.

Public affairs strategy and implementation

It is undoubtedly true that an effective PA strategy will start with, and depends on, sound issues analysis. However, beyond the issues analysis stage, the task of developing and implementing an effective PA strategy will normally revolve around developing an effective communication strategy to address the identified issues and challenges. While that communication strategy may comprise many different elements and target very specific stakeholders identified as key players in the issues to be addressed, the communication strategy design and implementation will tend to follow a very similar pattern and stages to those identified for other functions, which was examined in more detail in Chapter 4. In short, comprising:

- **Situation and stakeholder analysis** – examining trends, policies, and scenarios along with *identifying and prioritising the relevant stakeholder groups*
- **Objective setting** – identifying the intended short- and longer-term outcomes to be achieved
- **Message strategy development** – constructing the key messages to be communicated to the targeted stakeholders
- **Communication channel strategy** – examining and selecting the channels/ communication activities to be used to deliver the core messages to the targeted stakeholder groups
- **Implementation** of the selected communication tactics
- **Monitoring and evaluation** – assessing the effectiveness of the delivery and impact of the strategy – have opinions and/or behaviour changed, have the targeted policy initiatives moved in the desired direction, etc.

To be effective, any communication strategy needs very careful tailoring of the messaging to the different audiences, leveraging storytelling and compelling narratives to engage stakeholders. The agreed message strategy needs to be delivered effectively and in a timely manner which will often involve coordinating a number of communication channels, and not simply the traditional staple option of media relations. Indeed, as we have highlighted elsewhere, the media landscape has been transformed in recent years by the explosion of social media, which has been almost mirrored by an equally sharp decline in the more traditional print and broadcast media. Understanding how best to utilise the various media and activities available to PA/communication professionals to maximise the impact of any campaign undertaken is one of the core skills that communication professionals are expected to 'bring to the table', but needs to be continually honed and updated.

Sometimes the use of both conventional and social media channels is just not appropriate for PA. This may be especially true when dealing with a potentially highly sensitive issue for PA and/or when the campaign's success hinges on reaching out to quite senior political figures who it is difficult to reach through conventional media channels. In such cases, it may mean that the public affairs strategy requires a very 'customised approach'. This might take the form, for example, of orchestrating one-to-one lobbying meeting with key influencers and political figures that might only be achieved with the involvement of the most senior management. In such cases, the role of PA is largely one of orchestrating the meetings and ensuring the senior management members are well-briefed in order to engage effectively with the targeted political figures and communicate the key messages to them.

Where the PA strategy does involve a significant element of political lobbying whether by the organisation's own management or PA team or professional lobbyists, it is crucial that such activity is conducted transparently and ethically to avoid any accusation of misrepresentation or inappropriate inducement or worse, corruption.

The public affairs case study (see Box 10.3) illustrates how the public affairs function became the problem-solving 'troubleshooter' for the UK water company – analysing the problem in hand, developing a strategy and delivering a workable plan which achieved a win-win solution for all stakeholders.

Public affairs evaluation

In many senses, the success of PA strategies and campaigns can be assessed simply in terms of whether the intended outcomes were achieved – whether the targeted legislation was adopted or denied, or the extent of issues resolved. However, as with other areas of PR/communication work, it is not always easy to establish a direct causal relationship between the PA campaign activity and the changes in legislation or other actions/ behaviours targeted. As with other areas of communication, careful monitoring of activities and reactions, and collection of feedback and other data can at least begin to offer a meaningful insight into how successful the PA activity proved in shaping the intended outcomes desired. Such careful monitoring and data collection enables evaluation to advance beyond simply presenting media coverage or other communication process measures.

Box 10.3 A public affairs strategy in practice – how a UK private water company's public affairs function harnessed issues management to stem deep reputational damage

A major UK water company that was under pressure from the regulator to make its charging mechanisms more environmentally fair significantly increased surface water charges (the cost of collecting and treating rainwater) to sports clubs, churches, and charities whilst reducing charges to larger businesses. Some of these groups had previously paid little or nothing towards the costs of capturing rainwater and felt aggrieved at the increases to their bills, compared to their ability to pay. They were highly vocal and organised in their criticism of the company's new charging rates through their MPs, Government, and the media – resulting in sustained haemorrhaging of the organisation's reputation. As a result, the water company's senior management felt highly pressurised and challenged.

The public affairs function stepped in and played a key role in helping to overcome what had become a major crisis for the company – proposing a strategy to listen to and record its detractors' criticisms, meaningfully engage with them whilst at the same time engaging with the regulator, the Environment Agency, and the Government to explore a solution. This strategy involved a series of one-to-one meetings with sports associations, church organisations, and charities, as well as 'Round Table' events, at which key stakeholder views were listened to – resulting in a better understanding of each other's grievances and their root causes. Responding to these pressures, the Water Minister subsequently changed the relevant legislation – enabling sports clubs, churches, and charities to be charged at a much more affordable rate whilst protecting the environment which met the Environment Agency's expectations. Previously, the legislation did not allow the company to discriminate its charging practices between non-profit and commercial customers. What this case example illustrates is that public affairs can often go well beyond basic media relations activity and may involve high-level discussions with senior management to advise and even persuade them to adopt courses of action or changes in policy in order to respond to potentially damaging external pressures and threats.

The future of public affairs

PA like all other communication disciplines is experiencing the impact of a number of significant changes in recent years that are continuing to reshape the communication environment and working practices. Not the least being the increasing role of artificial intelligence and digitisation of the communications field, which raised questions about how organisations will utilise these new technologies and what role communication professionals will play going forward. Some commentators have suggested that these new technologies and especially AI will remove the need for many of the technical and creative skills that human communicators have cultivated and prided themselves on possessing. In the PA field, will AI and large data crunching computer power remove the need for human issues analysts and communication planners, reducing corporate communication and PA to an automated digitally driven chatbot-type of systems? The counterargument is that while AI and machine learning can perhaps readily handle the more routinised data processing and information dissemination, the need for skilled and experienced human intervention in analysing the subtleties of human and organisational relationships and handling their interaction is unlikely to be replaced by digital services at least in the foreseeable future. Organisations that overlook this need for an experienced human professional at the heart of their communication strategy may do so at their peril.

References and additional reading

A Guide to Public Affairs – PubAffairs – The Leading Public Affairs Network. publicaffairsnetworking.com

Moss, D.A., McGrath, C., Tonge, J. and Harris, P. (2012). Exploring the management of the corporate public affairs function in a dynamic global environment. *Journal of Public Affairs*, *12*(1), 47–60.

Public affairs: A strategic approach to building relationships with your communities of influence. Local Government Association. https://www.local.gov.uk/

Additional reading

Journal of Public Affairs

Harris, P. and Fleisher, C. (eds.) (2005) *The handbook of public affairs*. London: Sage.

11 International public relations

Barbara DeSanto

Box 11.1 Essentials summary

Modern-day public relations practice has developed post-WWII largely in the Western world, primarily the UK and the US. As such, it has social-cultural-political characteristics representative of these areas. During the past two to three decades, these ideas and practices have spread internationally resulting in public relations becoming recognised as an international discipline and practice. While many of the core disciplinary ideas and practices remain broadly common, academics and professionals have had to adapt the underpinning ideas and practices to take account of the local environment conditions and constraints whether in terms of societal culture, media systems, regulatory frameworks, and regulatory controls. This chapter explores how these international/global considerations have shaped the way PR thinking and practice have evolved to reflect these influences on the international/global stage.

Moving beyond domestic borders to a new region, country, and/or culture requires more than just translating one native language into another native language. While language differences are often the first thought in international work, understanding and adapting to the values, beliefs, and behaviours of another culture are the determinants that generally predict success or failure, for example, in terms of the success of an organisation's expansion of business operations into new international markets. This chapter highlights the factors/considerations communicators need to take account of/or develop to help their organisations become competent/highly effective international/global entities.

DOI: 10.4324/9781003129004-14

A definition for the terms often used interchangeably in international/global practice is useful in understanding the complexities of international practice:

- 'Global' is the term used to describe the umbrella – the overarching function – of public relations around the globe. Most countries in the world now recognise the term 'public relations' as a global concept.
- 'International' is the term to describe the specific type of public relations practised in specific geographic areas, such as countries and regions, of the world.
- 'Multicultural' is the term used to describe the potential mix of cultural and social characteristics of specific groups of people who can be residents of one physical country, or residents with the same cultural and social history within a country or that spans several countries' established boundaries because of physical and/or historical features.

Traditional business practice tends to explore the business/market environment in terms of a four-dimensional STEP framework, exploring the (S)social, (T) technical, (E)economic, and (P)political forces shaping a business's industry marketplace. While these STEP variables offer a basis for understanding generic business foci, when considering international expansion across regional or national border highlights the need for a further variable: cultural analysis. As organisations expand their operations across borders, they find the people they need to interact with, whether customers, employees, suppliers, distributors, or government regulators may operate under very different cultural values, motivations, and associated behaviours than those found in the organisation's 'domestic' home market/country. Thus, the organisation needs to add a 'cultural lens' to the traditional STEP framework. As is explored later, other similar frameworks have also been advanced over time to help analyse international environmental differences that may demand a reshaping of the PR/ communication strategy when deployed in specific international locations.

Who are the key stakeholders that international practitioners typically focus on?

- International and culturally specific lawmakers and regulators and regulatory bodies;
- National/regional local government bodies and governmental bodies with oversight of the organisation's field of work;
- International investors and banking and finance systems;
- The ownership and structure of different media systems, including global, international, regional, and local information channels, with additional attention to social media practices;
- Multilingual speakers with advanced understanding of and experience in locally specific languages;

- Key market segments and consumers – here analysed in terms of how their local cultural sensitivities might affect usage and demand for the products/services on offer;
- International/local special interest groups/pressure groups related to issues that are relevant to the organisation's operations. See Chapter 9 for an insight into just how complex this analysis of potential stakeholder groups can prove when looking to communicate internationally. Box 11.2 illustrates the potential complexity of stakeholder analysis for PR in a hugely diverse country like India.

Box 11.2 International stakeholder analysis for targeting in India

For any consumer-related campaign targeting the Indian market, whether, for a consumer product, healthcare, or other household-related product or service, the starting point for communicators is recognition of India's huge 1.3 billion population. To narrow the targeting and then adapt the communication strategy, communicators would need to examine such considerations as:

- There are some 22 official languages spoken in different regionals of India
- The caste system still creates large divisions in society
- Similarly, there are significant religious divisions within Indian society with the largest affiliations being Hinduism, Muslim, and Christian sections
- Politically, there are some 28 states and 8 union territories each having separate divisions and administrative districts

What are the key issues that international PR will encounter/need to address?

The notion and existence of cultural differences between people from different cultures and countries are widely recognised in general terms, including differences in tastes, attitudes towards work and lifestyle, as well as behaviour towards others. However, a practical framework is needed to develop effective communication strategies that recognise and address these differences. Here, one of the earliest and most enduring frameworks is Geert Hofstede's (1980) 'Cultural Dimensions Theory'. Here, Hofsted identified six key dimensions of culture (see Table 11.1), which he argued were manifest in terms of differences in personalities and behaviours. From a communication perspective, practitioners understand that cultures themselves have different personalities.

Table 11.1 Hofstede's Cultural Dimensions

Dimension	*Definition*
Power distance index	Refers to inequality of power between/among different groups of people
Individualism versus Collectivism	Refers to the strength of ties among/between people and communities
Masculinity versus Femininity	Refers to the different roles men and women are recognised for
Uncertainty avoidance index	Refers to how well anxiety/risk is handled in different cultures and situations
Long-term versus Short-term orientation	Refers to the time orientation that cultures operate in
Indulgence versus Restraint	Refers to the degrees of gratification a society allows its individuals

Source: A summary of Hofstede, G. (2011). 'Dimensionalising Cultures: The Hofstede Model in Context'

Hofstede developed this framework from data gathered from a large-scale study of more than 1,000 of the U.S. company IBM's workforce based in more than 50 countries. This and a follow-up study in 2010 (Hofstede and Minkov) led to the six cultural dimensions used today.

In subsequent research, Hofstede and others were able to link these cultural dimensions to other variables, including geographic proximity, shared language and dialects, similar religious beliefs, common philosophical influences, and political system orientations and variations. Thus, for example, where people live close to one another, they are likely to interact, share thoughts, and understand each other's ways of doing things. Where countries share a common language, they will often exhibit similar cultural values (Hofstede 2011).

International scholar Zaharna (2001) adapted Hofstede's cultural dimensions into more specific categories of country profiles, cultural profiles, and communication components. Sriramesh and Vercic (2003) added levels of development in four infrastructure profiles, which can impact any PR communication strategy.

Most recently, Molleda and Koehhar (2019) describe the main issues of countries using global/international public relations:

- Attracting foreign investment;
- Gaining political clout;
- Increasing tourism;
- Increasing development for social change;
- Achieving membership in the international community of nations.

Table 11.2 compares the three frameworks of the components these international researchers identified.

Table 11.2 Selected International Public Relations Frameworks

Zaharna	*Sriramesh and Vercic*	*Molleda and Kochhar*
Country profile • Infrastructure features • Political system • Economic system • Mass media system • Legal system • Social system Cultural profile • Low-high context variations • Monochromic/polychromic variations • Individual/collective variations • Future/past influences • Linear/non-linear orientation Communication components • Verbal/non-verbal • Visual • Group dynamics • Decision-making practices (R. Zaharna (2001). *Public Relations Review* (27)2, 135–148)	Infrastructure profile • Political development • Economic development level • Level of activism • Legal system (K. Sriramesh & D. Vercic eds. (2003). The Global Public Relations Handbook, Lawrence Erlbaum & Associates, Mahwah, NJ).	• Social/cultural traditions • Political systems • Economic development levels • News practices and infrastructure • Nature of types of activism • Laws and regulations (J.C. Molleda & S. Kochhar (2019). Global and Multicultural Public Relations, Wiley-Blackwell, Herndon, VA).

Although taking slightly differing starting points, the common themes among these three frameworks is that they address different aspects of cultural/social/media systems, and the infrastructure of different countries, including the political, economic, and technological environments. Collectively, they all focus attention on how analysis of these infrastructure variables can help identify what might be strategically important issues and challenges for any global/international business and PR practice.

What are the typical PR/communication tactics that can be deployed?

- One of the most important contributions the PR/communication function can make in supporting the development of international business is in terms of the business/market intelligence gathering work conducted as part of its *boundary spanning* role that enables organisations to explore the customs, languages and dialects, and social nuances that are key to creating meaning common goals and objectives;
- Then, examining carefully the relevant technological and ubiquitous explosion of digital and social media as well as the availability and effectiveness of traditional media channels in different countries which are critical to planning any communication campaign
- In principle, the design and development of a PR/communication campaign for any particular country region involve broadly common steps and processes wherever the programme is delivered [see Chapter 4 Strategy and Planning]. What might be very different is the specific targeting and message development that will need to be adapted to the social-cultural standards and traditions, media structures and availability, and regulatory environment in each targeted country/region. How such adaptation might be manifest is illustrated in the following mini-case example in Box 11.3

Box 11.3 Two American soft drinks make hard landings

Two international companies that failed internationally due to cultural differences are Pepsi and Coca-Cola. According to Kwintessential, both beverage giants faced some significant cultural/communication issues when first moving into the Chinese markets. Coca-Cola named their product a Chinese phrase that would sound like the original name.

However, this new phrase translated to 'Bite the Wax Tadpole'. This didn't go over well. Pepsi brought a new slogan to the Chinese market. It was 'Pepsi brings you back to life'. Unfortunately, the phrase translated to 'Pepsi brings your ancestors back to life'. Both companies had to revamp significant elements of campaigns for the Chinese market.

See Leonard (2019).

The importance of cultural and national sensitivities

- One of the most difficult challenges in international/global PR/communication management comes when we have genuine global organisations that want to communicate consistent 'brand/ reputation' messages around the world. Here, communicators may face some very significant challenges in adapting and translating core messages and perhaps imagery across international boundaries without compromising the central message/values that the organisation wishes to communicate without transgressing localised cultural sensitivities that might damage local perceptions of the organisation. This is where highly skilled and experienced international communicators are needed and demonstrate their value in adapting communication to avoid upsetting local tastes and sensitivities while not necessarily compromising the integrity of the message that the organisation wants to communicate. An example of this type of globally adapted communication strategy is outlined in Box 11.4.

Box 11.4 BMW sings the blues

German car manufacturer BMW made the marketing mistake of improperly using the national anthem of the United Arab Emirates in one of its car commercials. The ad displayed the 'Al Ain' Football Club singing the anthem and then breaking into a run towards several BMW cars when they heard the sound of the engine. Although the brand was trying to arouse intense emotion, it evoked rage instead of passion. Emiratis found it incredibly offensive that the car company suggested its cars were more important than the national anthem. The company explained that its intent was never to offend, and it soon replaced the ad with a less offensive version. See Schooley (2017).

- Where appropriate, employing local practitioners or local PR agencies from all relevant international locations can help avoid often unintentional, but highly damaging and/or embarrassing mistakes. For example, the choice of something as simple as colour schemes and forms of packaging might prove a cultural mistake in other cultures. Similarly, gestures, words, and graphics all have cultural connotations.

International PR evaluation

In previous chapters, we have highlighted the challenge of measuring the true impact of PR/communication campaigns, particularly in terms of attributing observed change to the specific PR communication activity undertaken. Equally, as has been highlighted, it is not always possible to disentangle the impact of PRE/Communication from all the other influences that might affect a particular outcome or particular decision/behaviour on the part of identified stakeholder groups. What has been emphasised earlier is the importance of not treating the measurement of media coverage (whether traditional or social media) – the process of communication, with the outcome/impact of that communication on the target publics. Such warnings are all the more important and relevant when seeking to assess the success of international/global communication where often the investment involved is much greater than domestic communication campaigns and hence there may be a temptation to look to and accept more readily available media output measures than commit the resource that may be needed to complete meaningful impact/outcome measurement across international borders.

Summary

This chapter has examined the complexity and challenges of developing PR communication across and between international and global borders. Public relations professionals with experience in different cultures and environments can assess the important nuances of the cultures/countries different from their own native ones, and create meaningful messages and campaigns that respect these differences.

References and additional reading

Culbertson, H.M. and Chen, N. (eds.) (1996). *International public relations: A comparative analysis*. Mahwah, NJ: Lawrence Erlbaum Associates.

Hofstede, G. (2011). Dimensionalising cultures: The Hofstede model in context. *Online Readings in Psychology and Culture*, *2*(1), https://doi.org/10.9707/2307/2307-0919.1014

Leonard, K. (February 5, 2019). *Examples of public relations campaigns*. [Accessed on 17 February 2024] https://smallbusiness.chron.com/examples-public-relations-campaigns-10110.html

Schooley, S. (2017). Lost in translation: 13 international marketing fails. *Businessnewsdaily.com*. [Accessed on 23 October 2023].

Sriramesh, K. and Vercic, D. (eds.). (2003). *The global public relations handbook: Theory,research, and practice*. Mahwah, NJ: Lawrence Erlbaum Associates.

Zaharna, R. (2001). 'In-awareness' approach to international public relations. *Public Relations Review*, *2*(27), 135–148.

Additional reading

Arthur, W. and Page Society. Teacher's guide to international/global public relations. The Arthur W. Page Society for Ethics and Integrity in Public Communication, Donald P. Bellisario College of Communication, Penn State University, State College, PA. [Accessed on 28 September 2023] https://bellisario.psu.edu

Molleda, J.C. and Kochlar, S. (2019). *Global and multicultural public relations*. Herndon, VA: Wiley-Blackwell.

12 Public relations and social media

Rebecca Dickenson and Natalie Elvin

Box 12.1 Essentials summary

This chapter examines the changing media landscape, the rise of digital platforms, and the power of social media. We explore the public's role in shaping discourse, and how to maximise your content channels to deliver the best PR outcomes.

Changing media landscape

As has been acknowledged elsewhere within this book, public relations is not entirely preoccupied with media relations work. Indeed, some accounts of public relations work might seem to imply it is almost synonymous with media relations. This said, there is little denying the fact that for most public relations departments or agencies, media relations remains the most important channel used to communicate with their target publics. What has undoubtedly transformed the traditional work of media relations has been quite marked changes in the media landscape, driven in part at least, by the way in which people consume media, not just in the UK, but globally.

The media landscape

The significant transformation in media landscape in recent years has seen a steady decline in traditional media outlets reflecting the marked decline in traditional media consumption. Traditional media, once the dominant force in information dissemination, has faced numerous challenges, particularly with the rise of digital platforms.

Print circulations continue to decline significantly and there has also been a substantial reduction of journalist headcounts across newspapers and magazines. Many publications have been forced to adapt to the changing times by

DOI: 10.4324/9781003129004-15

implementing cost-cutting measures and restructuring their operations. The economic challenges posed by declining print revenues have led to the downsizing of newsrooms and magazine staff.

In recent years, media outlets have had to diversify and adapt to remain relevant and viable. While some print publications will always have a role in shaping public discourse, the survival and success of most media outlets increasingly depend on their ability to navigate the dynamic digital landscape.

Embracing the digital revolution has become imperative, with online platforms serving as a lifeline for media organisations looking to connect with a broader and more tech-savvy audience, whilst retaining their traditional, often older, audience profile.

New platforms and evolving audiences

The digital boom has seen the emergence and rapid growth of a new wave of media platforms. In the pre-digital era, newspapers, radio, and TV were the primary sources of news for the public. People relied on these established channels for their daily dose of news. However, the digital revolution has unlocked unparalleled accessibility and immediacy, giving people the power to consume information whenever it suits them, from a wealth of sources (e.g. see Brown, 2009; Waddington, 2012). While on the surface, mobile and Internet access might appear to have become almost universally present within society and especially amongst younger age groups, some commentators have pointed to signs of a growing digital divide within society, with a class of socially and economically deprived individuals and families who are simply unable to afford the Internet or mobile phone costs needed to access these new social media channels on a regular basis. Arguably, these divisions, in terms of access to social media, have been triggered and then exacerbated by the impact of Covid and the spiralling inflationary costs felt across all sections of society, but amongst the poorest strata in particular. These arguments aside, there little denying the pervasive impact of social media on society today.

From new social media channels and digital news websites to podcasts, video and streaming services, new information sources have become integral components of the contemporary media landscape, giving people the opportunity to consume [or not] from more sources than ever before.

According to research released in October 2023 by the Reuters Institute, only a fifth of respondents now prefer to start their news journey on a news website or app. Particularly with younger age groups (18 to 24), there is a much weaker connection to 'news brands' than ever before, with consumers preferring to access news via 'side-door' routes such as social media or search.

Social media platforms, in particular, have played a pivotal role in reshaping how news is disseminated, consumed, and interacted with. It has become one of the most used platforms for gathering news, political viewpoints, and opinions particularly amongst younger sections of the population, not just in the UK but increasingly so globally.

However, for most of the social media platforms, the key challenge is not just in attracting users and consumers but retraining them in the face of new competitors. Here, for example, Facebook, once the dominant force for news consumption, has seen a decline in its influence on journalism, with dynamic, video-based platforms like TikTok and YouTube rising in popularity, thanks to their real-time, visually engaging content style (see Box 12.2 for recent trends in social media usage).

Box 12.2 Trends in social media usage

Social media growth

There are 4.8 billion social media users worldwide, representing 59.9% of the global population and 92.7% of all Internet users.

People use an average of 6.6 different social networks each month.

As of April 2023, the most used social media platforms, ranked by global active users, were Facebook, YouTube, WhatsApp, Instagram, and WeChat.

Nearly 64.5% of social media users receive breaking news from Facebook, Twitter, YouTube, Snapchat, and Instagram instead of traditional media.

Introduction to social media relations

In light of the sea change in the media landscape away from more traditional forms and towards digital platforms, increasingly businesses have recognised the need to embrace social media as a priority channel for PR activities.

Platforms like LinkedIn, Facebook, Instagram, X, and TikTok allow brands to bypass the 'gatekeepers' of traditional news sources to reach their audiences.

Self-publishing and thought leadership

Organisations are no longer held back by the potentially huge costs associated with advertising or investing time and energy into pitching stories to editorial journalists.

Using their social media accounts as a self-publishing tool, businesses are able to control to a large degree the messages they share with their audience and have full and final say over what is published.

'Thought leadership' (see Box 12.3) is also a valuable tool for businesses to build a strong brand and become a voice of authority in their fields. Sharing insights and opinion pieces on industry trends, thought leadership inspires readers through research-driven content that offers educational value through the knowledge, expertise, and experience of the author.

Box 12.3 Thought leadership

What is thought leadership?

In simple terms, thought leadership is the sharing of knowledge and ideas that show a person or a team of people to experts in a particular topic or field.

Thought leaders establish themselves as influencers among their audiences by offering inspiration and guidance. They will often share their perspectives on key industry trends, for example. Their content will often also offer advice and guidance underpinned by their experience and expertise.

Curation is also a characteristic of a strong thought leader, often sharing resources their audience might be unaware of and recommending connections to other people or services.

Some thought leaders also position themselves as challengers. They will offer new and alternative viewpoints, and share updated success metrics, frameworks, and definitions.

Thought leadership content is meant to spark discussion and position the person or organisation as a go-to source of knowledge.

Creating content strategy

Social media only works for businesses when it is supported by a strong overarching *content strategy*. A brand's content strategy is concerned with the planning, creation, delivery, and monitoring of content. Simply put, content refers to any useful and effective material about a particular topic. This content could be in the form of writing, audio recordings, videos, images, photographs, artwork, or another type of media.

Businesses will then share this content across their channels. And the way they plan out and share this content forms their content strategy.

Consistent, regular, good-quality content is essential for ensuring you have enough material to use on social media. Due to time and budget constraints, most businesses will tend to focus on just one or two of the following common content types for regular publishing:

- Blog posts
- E-books
- Podcasts/vodcasts
- Videos
- Webinars
- Email campaigns
- News articles
- Case studies
- Guides

High-quality content is vital for maintaining a brand's reputation, so significant thought should be put into production, including assets such as professional photography and video footage, audio and video editing, and professional copywriting and design.

Of course, the need for a strong content strategy predates the advent of social media and is nothing new. In this respect, the core principles have not changed much, but organisations are now able to self publish, rather than relying on more traditional avenues for their PR activities.

Box 12.4 also summarises how the arrival of AI technologies is impacting on content creation.

Box 12.4 Using AI

A word on AI for content creation

Leveraging AI writing apps can significantly cut down content planning and creation. But beware – some tools produce factually inaccurate, bland writing that might save you time, but won't do much to engage your audience.

Use AI for

- Research and idea generation
- Article and blog post outlines
- Content strategy and social media post ideas

Don't use it for

- Final drafts that you simply copy and paste
- Facts and details that need to be accurate
- Customer research using sensitive data that hasn't been anonymised

Choosing the right channels

Initially, it can be tempting for businesses to throw everything at social media and start an account on all the channels available. However, unless a business has a huge marketing team, this approach quickly becomes unsustainable.

Instead, brands should look at their customer base and find out where they spend most of their time online. If, for example, their ideal customer avatar (ICA) only uses LinkedIn, then it would be a waste of time for the business to create TikTok videos.

For example, a CEO of an onboard retail payment terminal supplier for the railway industry might only use LinkedIn as their preferred social media platform. This could be to do with the large-scale B2B nature of the business. Customer research might suggest that the decision-makers this brand needs to reach spend most of their time on LinkedIn. Whereas a wellness coach working with first-time parents might choose to focus their efforts on Instagram.

In addition to its application in relation to brand strategy, social media has also been a useful tool across the broader spectrum of business stakeholder activity. LinkedIn groups can be used for employee CPD or investor relations, for example, X (formerly known as Twitter) is often used for news and updates, and Facebook groups and pages can be leveraged for community relations.

Content pillars for social media

Although it is a powerful tool for the delivery of content to support a company's brand strategy, it's important to recognise that social media can be deployed in many different ways by businesses (e.g. Noor -Al-Deen and Hendricks, 2013). Apart from employee comms and community and investor relations, it can also perform a powerful customer service function, and it has exciting possibilities in the form of social proof and user-generated content.

SaaS business (Software as a Service), Dubsado, has created a Facebook community group where users can collaborate and support each other. While the main activity comes from the users, Dubsado admin people are also active in the group, signposting resources and answering questions. While it doesn't replace the company's customer service team, it is a valued way for users to get quick answers to their questions which they then don't need to contact the Dubsado team about.

This kind of user-generated content, along with photos and videos of people using products, and testimonials and reviews, is a digital form of word-of-mouth.

Informed by a comprehensive overarching content strategy and supported by high-quality brand assets, most brands will plan their social media into topics known as '*content pillars*'.

These pillars will vary from brand to brand, but they will largely fall into two main categories: *approachability stories* and *authority stories*.

Authority stories are concerned with sharing posts that show that you know what you are doing. They include things like educational pieces, case studies, and customer testimonials. Authority stories help build trust among your audience.

Approachability stories help your audience to connect with you beyond your expertise. If, for example, you are an e-commerce brand selling beauty products in a saturated market, approachability stores will help you stand out. Sharing a behind-the-scenes post of one of your processes or crafting an opinion post about sustainability will help potential customers get the measure of the people behind the brand and decide if you're for them.

Self-publishing

As we have outlined earlier, the landscape of information dissemination has undergone a transformative shift. There is now a demand for real-time, authentic content, giving rise to a new era of self-publishing.

In this digital age, citizen journalists and content creators have assumed pivotal roles, reshaping the dynamics of news sharing on a global scale. The 24/7 appetite for information has turned individuals into information contributors, challenging the established norms of journalism and fostering a democratised approach to the creation and dissemination of messaging.

Citizen journalists

The rise of citizen journalism has changed the way in which news and information are collected, reported, analysed, and disseminated. It involves members of the public actively participating in the journalistic process. When events unfold, individuals armed with smartphones are often the first responders, capturing real-time footage and sharing breaking news before traditional media outlets have left the newsroom.

This immediacy and ground-level perspective has been particularly evident in major global events, such as Russia's invasion of Ukraine, where citizens documented the aftermath of attacks and living conditions. Similarly, during incidents like the shootings in Paris or the Tribe of Nova festival in Israel, citizen journalists provided first-hand accounts, offering an unfiltered glimpse into unfolding events.

However, the power wielded by citizen journalists comes with its own set of challenges. Unlike trained journalists, they lack formal regulation and oversight from industry bodies. This absence of monitoring can lead to distorted content that is opinionated and potentially influenced by unconscious biases. Instances of misinformation have surfaced, notably during the Covid-19 pandemic and the Israel/Gaza war, where unverified content rapidly spread, influencing public perception.

For public relations practitioners, navigating the landscape shaped by citizen journalism requires a strategic approach. Constant monitoring of digital sources is crucial, enabling quick responses and corrections to any misinformation that may impact a client.

Identifying influential citizen journalists within a specific sector becomes imperative, as their coverage often shapes public discourse. Keeping up to date with their content helps PR practitioners understand the issues being covered and allows for proactive engagement or crisis management as needed. Moreover, when seeking news for PR purposes, prioritising reliable and substantiated sources becomes paramount. This ensures that the information being utilised is accurate, reducing the risk of inadvertently amplifying misleading narratives.

Content creators and influencers

In a landscape that extends beyond breaking news and citizen journalism, a compelling opportunity emerges for PR practitioners. Content creators and influencers are now pivotal players in shaping the consumer decision-making processes (e.g. see Waddington, 2012).

These individuals, who harness a significant social media following, wield real influence, impacting not only the products we buy and services we use but also the causes we support and the life choices we make.

Unlike traditional forms of advertising, influencers on social media platforms like Instagram and TikTok possess dedicated followings of like-minded fans. They leverage their credibility to share information and recommendations that resonate with their values, prompting specific actions from their engaged audience. The power of influencers lies not only in their ability to reach a vast audience but also in their role as authentic voices within their niche (see Box 12.5).

Box 12.5 Influencer types

- Mega influencer – 1M + followers
- Macro influencer – 100,000 to 1M followers
- Micro influencer – 1,000 to 100,000 followers
- Nano influencer – Fewer than 1,000 followers

When selecting an influencer to work with, it is important to consider quality over quantity. It may seem logical to aim for macro or mega influencers with the largest number of followers, but it is often the micro influencers who hold the most benefit for brand and business collaborations.

Although they may have smaller follower numbers, micro influencers tend to have higher engagement rates as their followers are more actively engaged and involved, leading to more meaningful interactions. This can be an extremely cost-effective way to build brand awareness and audience engagement.

For example, in the realm of food influencers, it would be more beneficial to work with an influencer that has under 100,000 followers but an engagement rate of over 5%, rather than going for a mega influencer like Jamie Oliver, who has 9.8M followers but an engagement rate of 0.08%.

Most influencers are open and willing to collaborate with brands and businesses, often in exchange for a fee. This collaboration entails the promotion of goods, services, or causes that seamlessly align with the influencer's demographic and personal brand. The authenticity and relatability of influencers' content contribute to its impact, making third-party advocacy more powerful than traditional advertising.

Recommendations from influencers are often perceived as more authentic and valued by their already-engaged audience, fostering a sense of trust that can be challenging to achieve through conventional advertising.

Approaching influencers as a PR practitioner requires a nuanced understanding of their profile and their audience before initiating contact. It is essential to ensure that the brand, product, service, or cause being pitched aligns seamlessly with the influencer's content and values. Personalising and tailoring the approach to align with the influencer's identity is also crucial.

When collaborating with influencers, providing a clear brief with objectives and key messages is imperative. This ensures that the influencer understands the campaign's goals and can authentically incorporate them into their content. Successful influencer partnerships rely on the synergy between the brand and the influencer, emphasising shared values and mutual benefit. As influencers continue to play a central role in shaping consumer perceptions and choices, adeptly navigating these collaborations becomes an integral aspect of any contemporary PR strategy.

Importance of strategy

When you come to creating a strategy for your digital communications via social media, you need to make sure you incorporate three key areas: digital listening, self-publishing, and engagement.

Digital listening

A strong strategy should start with *digital listening*. This is the act of researching what your target audience is talking about online. It gives you an insight into what they will find interesting, which can give you a springboard for developing your content strategy.

Good digital listening means:

- You can get an idea of how your customers feel about your brand. What do they think of the quality of your service or products? Are they excited about new announcements?
- You can offer support to customers who have perhaps used their social media account to vent about a problem they have.
- You can monitor campaigns and identify new opportunities for new products and services by tracking keywords and hashtags across the channels.
- You can also research your competitors and monitor industry trends to zero in on popular talking points (see Box 12.6 for an example of the use of digital listening).

Box 12.6 Aldi's #FreeCuthbert campaign

When Marks & Spencer launched an IP claim against Aldi's Cuthbert caterpillar birthday cake, the social media back and forth that followed was a masterclass in digital listening.

Aldi undoubtedly used social listening as a key step in the process of developing witty, meme-riddled responses to the ongoing legal action. Their PR team managed to turn a potentially very damaging event into a social media triumph.

By understanding their audience, they were able to be creative with their content, and although they lost the legal battle in court, it could be said they made a huge win in terms of public opinion.

There are many tools on the market that businesses can use to track conversations and trends taking place on social media channels. Tools such as 'Sprout Social', 'Brandwatch', and 'BuzzSumo' can be used to track conversations connected to your brand across different social networks. You can use them to identify trends, understand audience preferences, and pinpoint business opportunities.

In addition to paid tools that span a range of platforms, there are also quite useful features that are native to the platforms themselves. The built-in advanced search tool in X (previously known as Twitter) is a great resource for tracking conversations with a range of filters that can narrow your searches and allow you to zero in on specific accounts, keywords, and hashtags.

Google Alerts and Answer the Public also offer free basic social listening functions. Answer the Public offers insights on search volumes and associated search terms. Google Alerts is a free service that means you can monitor brand names, topics, and particular keywords.

Self-publishing

Businesses use self-publishing on social to broadcast to their followers. They will post messages using either video, images, or text-based posts to share knowledge, insights, updates, or news with their online networks.

Although self-publishing on social media gives businesses much more control over their messaging, it's worth remembering that only a small fraction of their audiences will see their organic posts.

On Instagram, for instance, only around 3–4% of an account's followers will see any given post. On Facebook, it's lower still – approximately 2%. With this in mind, it's important to share content regularly and consistently. Social media posting falls into two categories: *creation and curation.*

Content creation refers to posts created by the account. So this would be original imagery, graphics, videos, and text-based posts shared with their audience sharing news, insights, and education content.

Content curation, on the other hand, refers to the sharing of content created by other accounts. A business might choose to build up a list of complementary accounts whose content they regularly share. In this way, they can show a commitment to their industry by liking and sharing others' content.

Content curation is most effective when the account sharing the post adds to the conversation in some way. Shared posts accompanied by useful comments, or a different take that furthers discussion and sparks debate tend to be favoured by the algorithms. Whereas simply sharing others' posts without adding your own views doesn't seem to get as much reach.

We should point out here that the algorithms change all the time and what works one month might not work at all the next. So, it's a good idea to keep abreast of the latest updates and announcements from each of the platforms.

Engagement

Social media engagement is anything that carries on a 'conversation' via a post made from an account. So, this could be liking, commenting, and sharing posts that are published on a platform.

There's an ongoing tug of war between the social media platforms and the content creators using their platforms. The platforms want you to stay for as long as possible and consume more content. Content creators want to funnel followers off to their websites or email sign-up forms where they can better control their audience and turn them into leads that then convert to sales. As a result, users tend to get rewarded by the platform if they engage more. If you stay on Instagram after you have posted, and comment on others' posts, it could go in your favour in terms of your reach.

It's an unspoken rule that for every post you publish, you should aim to engage with five posts by other people. But Instagram, for example, wants to see comments of more than just a few words. It wants to see meaningful comments that spark conversations and keep people on its platform for longer. If the social media algorithms can see that a post is getting a lot of discussion, they consider it useful and interesting and thus show it to more people. This is a good reason for lingering on the platforms after your posts have gone out. It's important to respond to the comments of your audience and make sure you're engaging. Not only will this lead to better relationships with customers and potential customers, it will also enhance your brand's reputation for responsiveness as well as pleasing the algorithm.

Measuring impact

All of the main social media platforms have native functionalities for measuring impact via detailed reporting which you can use to monitor a variety of metrics (see Philips and Young, 2009).

Meta Business Suite has analytics available so you can track your reach, engagement, and audience numbers across your Facebook and Instagram accounts. X (formerly Twitter) and LinkedIn also have similar reporting capabilities, as does TikTok.

Through native reporting or using third-party social media tools and software, marketing teams can keep a keen eye on data to make informed decisions about future content strategies. They can see the kinds of posts that do well, spark conversations, and generate that algorithm-friendly engagement that means their posts get an increased reach (see Box 12.7 for more insights into social media evaluation).

Box 12.7 Social media evaluation metrics

Likes, follows, and vanity metrics

It can be tempting for businesses to attach too much value to vanity metrics like the number of followers and likes on their posts. And while generally speaking, increased follower numbers are no bad thing and accounts should be looking to achieve a positive growth trajectory, they shouldn't be tempted to focus on quantity at the expense of quality.

While it's widely known that it is incredibly bad form to resort to black hat tricks like buying followers – a practice which can see your account shadow banned at best and closed down altogether at worst – brands should also beware of resorting to legitimate methods of arbitrarily boosting follower numbers.

Competitions and giveaways, for example, are a good way to quickly increase your follower numbers, but the value of those followers should be considered in the planning process.

If your giveaway offers a prize that has little to do with your business and is not attractive to your ideal customer, you could end up with the wrong kind of audience.

Although rapid inflations of follower numbers might offer that temporary dopamine boost as you ostensibly hit your KPIs, what you end up with is a disengaged audience who never convert.

It's far better to grow steadily by offering valuable content that will appeal to your target audience. That way you build up trust as your audience gets to know and like your business enough to make a purchase, sign up, donate, or whatever it is you want them to do.

Agility

If social media is a lead generation tool for businesses, it's important to take it seriously and analyse the data. For some organisations, their social media accounts are more of a business card. They get new business through other avenues. For example, large business-to-business (B2B) entities might get their business through their network of contractors or partnerships and rarely get any suitable enquiries through social media.

This is where social media functions more as a shop window. It's a reflection of the organisation's values, image, and identity. In this respect, it might not be seen as a priority to allocate much time and budget to social media activities and tracking and analysing metrics might not be seen as a priority. But for business-to-consumer companies (B2C) and business-to-small business (B2b), tracking and analysing social post performance need to be built into their strategy. If, for example, poll posts on LinkedIn get a lot of engagement with an organisation's ideal client avatar, social media managers might develop a strategy for incorporating more of these types of posts.

The trend in the past couple of years on social media has been more towards short-form videos as evidenced by TikTok's explosion in popularity and Instagram's reels post format. As a result, many brands are investing more in creating this kind of content in a bid to please the algorithms. But again, it is always better to tailor your posting strategy to your audience. If videos aren't what your audience engage in, it wouldn't be worth investing time and budget into creating them. As tempting as it is to jump on the latest trends, any successful social media strategy always needs to start with audience research.

Measuring your campaigns needs to be more than looking back at what you've achieved. It is important to analyse the data and use the learnings to shape future content strategies.

Summary

So the key lessons or takeaways from this relatively brief examination of the use of social media in PR context are as follows:

- The traditional media landscape has undergone significant transformation, marked by the decline of print circulations and the rise of digital platforms globally.
- Embracing the digital revolution is imperative for media organisations, as online platforms become crucial for connecting with diverse audiences, including tech-savvy and traditional demographics.
- Media outlets are diversifying to remain relevant, with new platforms such as podcasts, video, and streaming services becoming integral components of the contemporary media landscape.
- Social media platforms play a pivotal role in reshaping how news is disseminated, consumed, and interacted with, especially among younger populations globally.
- Businesses recognise the need to prioritise social media as a key channel for PR activities, using platforms like LinkedIn, Facebook, Instagram, and TikTok to reach their audiences directly.
- Social media allows organisations to control their messaging through self-publishing, and thought leadership on industry trends helps build a strong brand and authority.
- A strong content strategy, involving consistent, high-quality content creation, is essential for successful social media presence.
- Content creators and influencers on social media platforms wield significant influence, and collaborating with them strategically can be a cost-effective way to build brand awareness and engagement.
- Measuring impact through analytics tools, adapting to changing trends, and tailoring content strategies based on audience preferences are crucial for successful social media engagement in PR.

References and additional reading

Brown, R. (2009). *Public relations and the social web*. London: Routledge.

Noor Al-Deen, H.S. and Hendricks, J.A. (2013). *Social media and strategic communications*. London: Palgrave Macmillan.

Philips, D. and Young, P. (2009). *Online public relations: A practical guide to developing an online strategy in the world of social media.* London: Kogan Page.

Waddington, S. (2012). Share this: *The social media handbook for PR professionals*. London: John Wiley & sons.

Index

Note: Page numbers in *italic* indicate a figure and page numbers in **bold** indicate a table on the corresponding page.

Absolute Essentials of Strategic Management (Witcher) 42
Absolut Vodka 84
action phase, crisis 106–107; tactics/actions 107–109
Ahlstrand, B. **40**
Aldi's #FreeCuthbert campaign 141
American marketing association (AMA) 78
approachability stories 138
artificial intelligence (AI) technology 69; for content creation 136; impact on industry sector 25; public affairs (PA) and 121–122
asymmetrical communication 11, 20–21; *see also* communication
authority stories 138

Berg, H. 82
Bernays, E.L. 5, 6
BMW 129
boundary spanning role 13, 15, 22, 101, 128
brand ambassadors-influencer marketing 83–84
brand's content strategy 135
bridging role 22, 23
Broom, G.M. 7, 27
buffering role 22, 23

campaign: Aldi's #FreeCuthbert 141; communication 130; corporate communication (CC) 72, **73–74**; Dove #*The Selfie Talk* 85; public affairs (PA) activity 120
CC *see* corporate communication (CC)
Center, A.H. 7
Chaffee, E. **41**
Chartered Institute of Marketing (CIM) 78
Chartered Institute of Public Relations (CIPR) 81; Code of Conduct 53, 59; 'State of PR 2020/21' report 115
Christensen, L.T. 65
citizen journalism 138–139
CMACIE model 37, 46–49, *47,* 102
Coca-Cola, in Chinese markets 128–129
Codes of Practice 51, 59
communication 10–11; asymmetrical *vs.* symmetrical 11; campaigns impact 130; employee 88–97; and in-house public relations (PR) departments 14–15; management of 5, 7, 9, 15, 65, 128–129; marketing 66; and MMR vaccine controversy, public health 20; organisational 11, 12, 66;

power of 55; types 55; *see also specific communications*
communication audit (CA) 97
communication strategy 37, 42; analytical skills 48; CMACIE framework 37, 46–49, *47*; conceptual frameworks and models 42; core idea 46; deployment 42; development 71; 'DNA' of 45–46; essential themes 42; evaluation 49; limited campaign planning model 46; linear planning models 43; planned programmes 42; positioning in 42; public affairs (PA) 119; purpose 42; RACE model 43, *43,* **44**; strategic planning 44; strategic thinking 44, 45
competencies, practitioner 29–30, **30**
composite role, practitioner 29
content creation 142; artificial intelligence (AI) for 136; strategy 135–136
content creators 139–140, 142, 145
content curation 142
content pillars 137–138
Coombs, T. 107, 109, 110
Cornelissen, J. 65
corporate communication (CC) 63; campaign activities 72, **73–74**; categories 65–66; economics 69; evaluation 72; features 66; government regulation 69; issues categories 68–69; managerial perspective 64; media and activity selection 71–72; message development 71; public affairs (PA) and 115; situation analysis 71; stakeholders for 66–68, **67**; strategy and implementation 70–72; supply chain/just in time 69; taxation levels 69; technological change 69; workforce retention/recruitment and skills 69
corporate reputation 70–71
Covid-19 pandemic 33–34, 115, 118, 139
craft public relations 21, *21,* 22
crisis: action phase 106–109; categories 101, **102**; communication team and action plans 105–106; financial services sector 103–104; Fujitsu Horizon software 103; government/private plan 108; planning process 103; preparation best practices 103–104; preparedness 104; stakeholder/issue analysis 104–105; types of 99–101, **102**
crisis management 99; physical accidents example 104; plan 101–102; post-crisis stage 102, *103*; pre-crisis stage 102, *103*; stages in 102–103, *103*
Cultural Dimensions Theory 125–126, **126**
Cutlip, S.M. 7, 48

'Day in the Life,' practitioner roles *33–34,* 33–34, *34–35*
DeSanto, B. 46, 108
De Witt, R. **40**
Dieselgate crisis 23
digital listening 141
digital platforms 132, 134
disciplinary communication strategy 71
discourse ethics **52**, 53, 59
'DNA' of communication strategy 45–46
Dove #*The Selfie Talk* campaign 85
Dozier, D.M. 27
Drucker, P. 38
duty ethics 53, **52**; *see also* ethics

employee communication: formal methods/activities 96; informal channels 97; two-way 94–95
employee engagement 91–93
engagement: employee 91–93; social media 142–143
engineering of consent 5, 6
environments, public relations (PR) 23–25, *24*

ethical decision-making 57–60, **58**
ethics: applications 59; codes of 55–56; definitions 50–51; discourse **52**, 53; duty 53, **52**; five pillars of 53; importance of 53–54; lobbying practices 113; in media relations 55–56, 59; personal 54, 58; principles 51, 53, 59; in public relation (PR) planning process 56, **57**; theories and perspectives 51–53, **52**, 59; utilitarian **52**, 53; virtue **52**, 53
Ethics of Care 54
Excellence study 44
external communication 90; *see also* internal communication (IC)

fast-moving consumer goods sector (FMCG) 14, 20, 79
Fawkes, J. 58
female career advancement 32–33
financial services sector crisis 103–104
Fombrun, C. 65
food influencers 140; *see also* influencers
Fujitsu Horizon software crisis 103
functional strategy 38; *see also* strategy

gender discrimination and practitioner roles 32–33
'glass ceiling' effect 32
global public relations (PR) 124, 126–128; *see also* public relations (PR)
Google Alerts 142
government/private crisis plan 108
Greenpeace 82
Gregory, A. 54
Grunig, J.E. 7, 11, 18, 19, 21, *45*
Grunig, L.A. 18, 21
guerilla marketing 84; *see also* marketing

Harlow, R. 6
Harris, T. 85
Herzberg, F. 92–93
Hofstede, G. 125–126
Hunt, T. 7, 19
hygiene factors 92–93

IC *see* internal communication (IC)
Iceland's palm oil initiative 81–82
industry sector 14; AI technology impact 25; environments by 24; and organisational influences 14–15
influencers: collaboration 140; content creators and 139–140, 145; food 140; macro and mega 139, 140; marketing strategy 83–84; micro 139, 140; types 139
informative communication 55, 59; *see also* communication
in-house public relations (PR) departments 14–15
integrated marketing communication (IMC) 65, 76, 84–85
internal communication (IC): active *vs.* passive role 96; challenges 88, 91, 93; definition 88–89; employees within organisational structure 93; evaluation 97; formal methods/activities 96; informal channels 96–97; issues 93, 95; key stakeholders in 90–91; organisational culture 93–94; problem scenarios 95; strategy and implementation 95–96; *see also* external communication
international public relations (PR) 15, 123–124; challenge in 15; Coca-Cola 128–129; communication tactics 127–130; cultural differences 128–129; evaluation 130; frameworks **127**; issues 125–128; key stakeholders 124–125; Pepsi 128–129; STEP framework 124
Israel/Gaza war 139

James, H. 55
Johnson, G. 38, **41**
Just Stop Oil 118

key stakeholders: in internal communication (IC) 90–91; international public relations 124–125; for public affairs (PA) 117; *see also* stakeholders
knowledge, practitioner 29–30, **30**, **31**
Kochlar, S. 126

Lampel, J. **40**
Leonard, K. 129
linear planning models, communication strategy 43
lobbying 113

management of communication 5, 7, 9, 15, 65, 129
management strategy **40–41**, 42, 48; *see also* strategy
managerial responsibility 29
manager role, public relations 26–29, *28*; day in the life 33–34, *34–35*; elements 28; technician *vs.* 28, *28*; *see also* manager-technician role dichotomy
manager-technician role dichotomy 26–29, *28*; day in the life *33–34*, 33, *34–35*
marketing 76–77; brand ambassadors-influencer 83–84; communication 66; dimensions/characteristics 79, **80**; Iceland's palm oil initiative 81–82; media relations tactic 83–84; multi-layered targeting in 24; newsjacking 83; P's of 78–79; product placement and endorsement 83; promotional tactics 82–84
marketing imperialism 86
marketing public relations (MPR) 85–86
McCarthy, J.E. 78
McVeigh, T. 100
media outlets 132, 133, 145
media relations: ethics in 55–56, 59; *vs.* public relations 132; tactic, marketing 83–84; *see also* social media
Meta Business Suite 143
Meyer, R. **40**
Mintzberg, H. 38, **40**, 44; 5Ps framework strategy 38–42, **39**, **40–41**
mixed motives model 21
MMR vaccine controversy 20
models of public relations (PR) 18, 19, *19, 21*; arguments 21–22; characteristics 19–20; effective 20–21; press agentry/propaganda 19; public information 20; two-way asymmetrical/symmetrical 20–21
Molleda, J.C. 126
Moreno, A. 30
Moss, D. 46, 114
motivation-hygiene theory 92–93
multicultural public relations (PR) 124; *see also* public relations (PR)

newsjacking 83
Newsom crisis typology **102**
NHS workforce statistics 90–91, **91**
Nolan Committee 113

Oklahoma City Bombing (1995) 100–101
one-way communication 11; *see also* two-way communication
organisational communication 66; ethical management 12; symmetrical model 11; *see also* communication
organisational culture 93–94
organisational strategy 38; *see also* strategy
Oxford Circus Tube station 84

P's of marketing 78–79; people 79; physical evidence 79; place 78; price 78; processes 79; product 78; promotion 78–79
PA *see* public affairs (PA)
Park, J. 11
Parsons, P.J. 53, 56, 58
Pepsi, in Chinese markets 128–129

personal attributes, practitioner 29–30, **30**, **31**
personal ethics 54, 58; *see also* ethics
persuasive communication 55; *see also* communication
Pettigrew, A.M. 94
political lobbying 113
post-crisis 102, *103,* 108; best practice 109–110
power imbalance 56
practitioner, public relations *see* public relations (PR) practitioner roles
PRCA's Professional Charter 59
press agentry/propaganda model 19
product placement and endorsement 83
professional bodies 50, 51, 59, 115
professional public relation 21, *21,* 22
public affairs (PA) 112; artificial intelligence and 121–122; business and government interest mediating role *114,* 115; campaign activity 120; case study 120–121; communication strategy 119; corporate communications 115; definitions 112–115; evaluation 120; explosive growth 115; future of 121–122; government policies/external events, consequence of 118; in highly regulated organisations 116–117; individualised approach 120; in-house *vs.* external professionals 116; issues/challenges for 117–118; key stakeholders for 117; organisational policies/actions, consequence of 118; stakeholder actions, consequence of 118; strategy 119–121; terminology 115; UK private water company 120–121
Public Affairs Council 113–114
Public Affairs Network 114
public information models 20
public relations (PR) 1; challenge for 5; communication campaigns impact 130; and communication strategy (*see* communication strategy); definition 5–9, 16; global 124; international (*see* international public relations (PR)); marketing and (*see* marketing); media relations *vs.* 132; models of (*see* models of public relations (PR)); multicultural 124; multiple operating environments 23–25, *24*; negative stereotypical themes in 11; perceptions of 5, 6, 13; practitioner (*see* public relations (PR) practitioner); purpose 18–19; reactive and proactive approach 13; and reputation 8; role of 22–25, *24*; scenarios in 12–13; scope of 23–24; and social media (*see* social media); traditional and globalisation industry 14; weakness and issue for 31–32
Public Relations and Communications Association (PRCA) 6
Public relations cases: International perspectives (Moss and DeSanto) 82
Public Relations Society of America (PRSA) 6, 7
public relations (PR) practitioner roles: (PR): communication types 55; competencies 29–30, 30; composite role 29; conceptual framework criticisms 29; definition 8–9; female career advancement 32–33; management perspectives 31–32; manager role 26–29, 28; public affairs (PA) 116; roles 26–27; skills, knowledge and personal attributes 29–30, 30, 31; technician role 26, 27, 28; work

patterns, practitioners role *33–34*, 33–34, *34–35*
publics 5; definitions 9–10; stakeholders *vs.* 10

RACE (Research, Action Planning, Communication, and Evaluation) model 43, *43,* 44; strengths and weaknesses 43, **44**
realised strategy 39; *see also* strategy
relationship-building/management 10
remote working 91–92
Repper, F. *45*
reputation: management 81; organisation 54; public relations (PR) and 8
respect of persons 53, 56
Ruck, K. 97

Schein, E.H. 94
Scholes, K. 38, **41**
self-publishing 138; on social media 142; tool 134–135
sequential planning process 44
seven-stage strategic planning model 44, *45*
situation analysis 71
skills, practitioner 29–30, **30**, **31**; *see also* public relations (PR) practitioner roles
social media 13, 27, 72; brand strategy 137; choosing right channels 137; content pillars 137–138; content strategy 135–136; digital listening 141; engagement 142–143; evaluation metrics 143–144; growth 134; measuring impact 143–145; platforms 133–135, 137; self-publishing 134–135, 142; strategy 140–143; thought leadership 134–135; tool 141; *see also* media relations
Sriramesh, K. 126, **127**
stakeholders: categories 68; for corporate communication (CC) 66–68, **67**; for crisis analysis 104–105; *vs.* publics 10; target public analysis 71
STEP framework, international public relations 124
strategic management model: CMACIE communications framework 46–48, *47*; seven-stage 44
strategic planning 39, 44; CMACIE framework 48; dynamic and resilient 43; perspective 43–44; seven-stage model 44, *45*
strategic thinking 39; in communication strategy-making 44, 45; strategic planning and 44
strategy: communication (*see* communication strategy); content creation 135–136; corporate communication (CC) 70–72; definition 37–38; evolutionary mode 48; functional 38; hierarchy 38; internal communication (IC) 95–96; Mintzberg's 5Ps framework 38–42, **39**, **40–41**; organisational 38; public affairs (PA) 119–121; *see also specific strategies*
symmetrical communication 11; two-way 94–95

technician role, public relations 26, 27; day in the life *33–34,* 33; manager *vs.* 28, *28*; *see also* manager-technician role dichotomy
Tench, R. 30
The Organisation for Professionals in Regulatory Affairs (TOPRA) 115
thought leadership 134–135
Tidwell, M. 23
traditional media 132, 145; *see also* social media
trust 8; employee 90
two-factor theory 92–93

two-way communication 5, 9, 11, 15, 77, 94–95; asymmetrical/ symmetrical models 20–21; *see also* communication; one-way communication

UK Local Government Association Network 114
UK private water company's public affairs 120–121
utilitarian ethics **52**, 53; *see also* ethics

Van Riel, C.B.M. 64, 65
Verčič, A.T. 90
Vercic, D. 126, **127**
virtue ethics **52**, 53; *see also* ethics
Volkswagon emissions scandal 23

Waddington, S. 8
Waters, J. **40**
White, C. 11
Whittington, R. 38, **41**
Witcher, B.J. 42
work patterns, practitioners role *33–34,* 33–34, *34–35*

Yaxley, H. 54

Zaharna, R. 126, **127**

For Product Safety Concerns and Information please contact our EU representative GPSR@taylorandfrancis.com
Taylor & Francis Verlag GmbH, Kaufingerstraße 24, 80331 München, Germany

www.ingramcontent.com/pod-product-compliance
Lightning Source LLC
LaVergne TN
LVHW050648100826
845148LV00011B/2033

* 9 7 8 0 3 6 7 6 5 3 4 0 8 *